REMEMBERING THE
BIG FOUR

THE LMS, LNER, SR AND GWR
IN PHOTOGRAPHS

PAUL HURLEY AND JEREMY SUTER

The
History
Press

Front cover images, clockwise from top left: GWR 4-6-0 6026 *King John*, Class King, at Warwick station in 1938; LMS 4-6-0 5589 *Gwalior*, Class Jubilee, at Hest Bank, Lancaster, in 1937; SR 4-6-2 21C14 *Nederland Line*, Class Merchant Navy, at Waterloo station in 1947; LNER 4-6-0 2834 *Hinchingbrooke*, Class B17, at Gorton Works in 1931.

Back cover image: LMS 4-6-2 6225 *Duchess of Gloucester*, Class Coronation, at Carlisle Citadel station in 1939.

Opposite: GCR 0-6-0 5656, Class J9. This Class-J9 locomotive was built by Neilson, Reid & Co. for the Great Central Railway (GCR). It was released into service in March 1891. In June 1912, it was given a boiler with a Belpaire firebox. In May 1925, it was a member of the LNER, and the locomotive was given the number 5656. It was also fitted with a flowerpot chimney at this time. It is seen here at Parkhead shed in Glasgow on 2 August 1925, with its new LNER number 5656. It carried this number throughout its service and was withdrawn in August 1934 after a service life of forty-three years, five months and two days. It was scrapped shortly after. No members of this class were saved.

First published 2022

The History Press
97 St George's Place, Cheltenham,
Gloucestershire, GL50 3QB
www.thehistorypress.co.uk

British Library Cataloguing in Publication Data.
A catalogue record for this book is available from the British Library.

ISBN 978 0 7509 9738 6

Typesetting and origination by The History Press
Printed in Turkey by IMAK

Trees for Life

CONTENTS

ABOUT THE AUTHORS

This will be the third railway book compiled by Paul Hurley for The History Press, following *Remembering Steam*, which commemorated the end of steam on British Railways (BR), and a follow-up book, *The Changing Railways of Britain*. He has also written twenty-six books on Cheshire and an award-winning novel.

Thanks to an early start with his father, Jeremy Suter has a lifelong passion for all things railway. As a result, he has amassed an extensive archive of railway images covering the UK and Irish railways. All images are from the Jeremy Suter Collection unless otherwise stated.

ACKNOWLEDGEMENTS

I would like to thank Ian Jenkins for allowing me to dip into his excellent website BRDatabase (www.brdatabase.info/) and David Woodward of the LNER Society for kindly sending me some ephemera for use in the book. Likewise, thanks to Peter Tatlow, president of the LMS Society, and Arnold Tortorella, secretary of the society. And, too, our wives, Rose and Pat, for their patience in what has taken us away from the front room for a considerable time. Also, our thanks to Amy Rigg, our publisher, and Alex Boulton for their help and advice. Then there are the photographers who, through the years, have left these old images to be enjoyed by future generations of steam-loving enthusiasts.

Paul Hurley

INTRODUCTION

It is now 100 years since Great Britain's railways were drawn together into four companies. They were known as the Big Four, but why?

In 1804 Richard Trevithick pioneered steam traction that was mobile on metal rails. Since the 1700s, wagonways had been used to feed mines and other industries using primitive, horse-drawn trucks on wooden rails, but Trevithick revolutionised this procedure with his steam-driven railway. Static steam boilers already existed to pump water and drive mills and coal mines, but with wheels and the ability to pull loaded wagons, here was a different use for the steam engine. Trevithick first used this new power on the Penydarren Tramroad in South Wales, and it worked. Steam-driven railway traction was born.

Trevithick's idea was to open colliery railways in the north-east, and designers such as Timothy Hackworth and John Blenkinsop designed the steam engines to haul the colliery wagons. They were, however, still primitive, but onto the scene came George Stephenson, who was to become known as 'the father of the railways'. Like the other engineers, he continued to work on locomotives for colliery use. He built the first line, the Stockton and Darlington Railway (S&DR), to link collieries near Shildon with Darlington and Stockton-on-Tees in the north-east, and it officially opened on 27 September 1825. However, Stephenson wanted this new power source to go further. There was more to it than designing engines to haul industrial products. If it could do that, why could it not carry paying passengers? He built the first inter-city line from Liverpool to Manchester in 1830; before it fully opened, the Rainhill Trials took place in 1829 to test his argument that steam-powered locomotives would be the best form of transport to run along it.

Stephenson's son, Robert, shared his father's passion for steam and entered a locomotive design of his own that he called *Rocket*. It went on to win the race, travelling at 30mph, although some of the shine was taken off as *Rocket* was the only entrant to finish! Stephenson's prize was worth £44,324 in today's money.

On 15 September the following year, the Liverpool and Manchester Railway (L&MR) opened. There was a race to get to Manchester, but sadly, the MP for Liverpool, William Huskisson, was struck by *Rocket*. He had travelled in a train pulled by *Northumbrian*, built for the Duke of Wellington, the prime minister, and driven by George Stephenson. When the train stopped for water and coal at Parkside station, Huskisson got out onto the adjoining track. *Rocket*, being driven by George Stephenson's assistant and future eminent railway engineer Joseph Locke, was travelling along that track and struck Huskisson, who later died of his injuries. There is a memorial to him at the accident site today; he was the first person to be killed in a railway accident.

Railway development moved quickly, from Trevithick in 1804, with his first high-pressure steam locomotive hauling a loaded train along a plateway in South Wales, to the Stephensons thirty years later, with their locomotives capable of hauling trains from Liverpool to Manchester. After this, Railway Mania started when vast profits could be made from investing in new railway companies. New lines spread like a spider's web across the country and abroad. Passenger trains that originally carried people in open trucks advanced through to comfortable and not-so-comfortable carriages that could be booked depending on the traveller's wealth. By 1846, 272 railway companies had received government approval. This included those at an early stage when shares were being sold to recoup the proposed cost of laying the tracks. It was a 'feeding frenzy' where the lucky ones could get fabulously wealthy, but some simply lost money.

Between 1845 and 1847, Parliament authorised the building of 8,000 miles of railway lines. Some worked, while some did not and were soon sucked into the larger companies, scrapped, or joined with others to form more successful business ventures, such as the L&MR's amalgamation with the Grand Junction Railway (GJR). This then joined with the Manchester and Birmingham Railway (M&BR) and the London and Birmingham Railway (L&BR). Then followed the final offering before amalgamation, the London and North Western Railway (LNWR). There was little in the way of organisation: some companies simply ran from town to town; some travelled the same route. Larger companies emerged, such as the Great Western and many, many others.

When the First World War broke out in 1914, the railway consisted of 20,000 miles of track owned by 120 companies. Going into the war, they were all controlled by the government and were worked hard. They came out battered and bruised, and soon it was decided that something had to be done. The country could not support so many diverse and, in some cases, overlapping companies. They would have to be brought together into a neat bundle of just four to cover England, Scotland and Wales and part of Northern Ireland.

The Railways Act 1921, also known as the Grouping Act, became law on 1 January 1923. After this, just four large companies, nick-named the 'Big Four', came into being after incorporating all but a few of the small companies. This meant that 120 separate railways were combined to make just four.

The London, Midland and Scottish Railway (LMS)
The LMS became the most significant commercial enterprise in the UK and second only to the Post Office in the number of people employed in Britain. It was also the biggest joint-stock company globally and the most extensive transport organisation in the world. Then there was the fact that it was also the most significant commercial enterprise in the British Empire. It was also the only member of the Big Four to operate in Northern Ireland, serving most of the province. The chief mechanical engineers (CMEs) were George Hughes (1923–25), Henry Fowler (1925–31), Ernest Lemon (1931–32), Sir William A. Stanier (1932–44) and Henry George Ivatt (1944–47).

The London and North Eastern Railway (LNER)
This was the second-largest operator after the LMS and owned 7,700 locomotives together with passenger and freight vehicles. It also held and inherited forty-two steam and turbine ferries, and river and lake steamboats, twenty-three hotels, eight canals, and twenty ports and harbours. The CMEs were Sir Nigel Gresley, who served from 1923 to his death in 1941, Edward Thompson, from 1941 to 1946, and Arthur Peppercorn from 1946 to nationalisation in 1948.

The Southern Railway (SR)
The Southern was the smallest of the Big Four, and its business catered more for passengers than freight. It became the first railway company to move extensively to electrification, including on the main lines. As time went on, it was the world's most extensive railway system powered by electricity and was also the wealthiest. The company replaced most of the stock that it inherited and had two CMEs, Richard Maunsell (1923–37) and Oliver Bulleid (1937–48).

The Great Western Railway (GWR)
The GWR was the only one of the Big Four to retain its name, which dated back to 1833. (In this book, I have marked pre-1921 GWR as 'original GWR'.) The company operated a series of bus routes and an airline, Railway Air Services. It also owned hotels and ports. There were just two CMEs under the Big Four, Charles Collett (1922–41) and Frederick Hawksworth (1941–47).

THE LONDON, MIDLAND AND SCOTTISH RAILWAY (LMS)

The prominent constituent companies incorporated into the LMS on amalgamation:

London and North Western Railway (LNWR) (amalgamated with the Lancashire and Yorkshire Railway (L&YR) as of 1922): a total of 2,667 miles (4,293km)
Midland Railway (MR): 2,171 miles (3,493km)
The Caledonian Railway (CR): 1,114 miles (1,794km)

Glasgow and South Western Railway (G&SWR): 493 miles (794km)
Highland Railway (HR): 506 miles (814km)
North Staffordshire Railway (NSR): 220 miles (355km)
The Furness Railway (FR): 158 miles (254km)

There were also thirty-eight other smaller companies amalgamated with the above or independent.

Locomotives in Companies Drawn into the London, Midland and Scottish Railway on Amalgamation

◄ G&SWR 4-6-4T 545, Class 540

First, we look at G&SWR locomotive No. 545, photographed new for a publicity shot. It had just two years before joining the new LMS. It was designed by railway engineer Robert Harben Whitelegg and built by the North British Locomotive Company in Glasgow in 1922, going into service in April. The locomotive did not work the metals for very long, just fourteen years and four months, before being withdrawn and scrapped in 1936. From 31 December 1925, it was an LMS engine bearing the number 15405.

◄ LNWR 4-6-0 66 *Experiment*, Class Experiment

No. 66 *Experiment* was built at Crewe Works in 1905 under CME George Whale and is seen here in Crewe station heading south fourteen years later. *Experiment* took the name and number of an earlier engine. The leader of the class of 105 locomotives, it was renumbered 5450 by the LMS but withdrawn and scrapped in July 1931. The rest of the class locomotives were all gone by October 1935.

► G&SWR 4-4-0 466, Class 153

Designed by Hugh Smellie for the G&SWR and built by Kilmarnock Works in 1886. Seen here at Dumfries shed in 1920, it had been renumbered 448 in June 1919 and would be an LMS member for a very short while. It received the LMS number 14138 in 1924, being withdrawn in April 1925.

▼ HR 4-4-0 95 *Strathcarron*, Class Strath

Here we have a David Jones-designed locomotive built in June 1892 by Neilson, Reid & Co. as a passenger locomotive. It is seen here at Elgin shed on 7 October 1926. Its original number was HR95, and in 1922 it received HR96A until amalgamation on entering the LMS, when it became 14274.

The number was not changed quickly as this photograph was taken in 1926 and it is still carrying its HR identity. Strathcarron, from which the locomotive took its name, is a hamlet in the Scottish Highlands. The locomotive was withdrawn in 1930.

▲ **HR 4-6-0 103, Class 'Big Goods'**
Here we find another Jones-designed locomotive, this time built by Sharp,
Stewart & Co. in Glasgow in September 1894. It is seen here passing through
Ballinluig station on an unknown date. It received the LMS number 17918 and
was withdrawn in 1933.

◄ CR 4-4-0 721 *Dunalastair*,
Class Dunalastair

Over now to another company to join the
Big Four, in this case, the CR. Here we have
one member of a beautiful class of fifteen
locomotives with the class leader *Dunalastair*.
It was designed by John F. McIntosh and built
by St Rollox Railway Works in Glasgow, going
into service in 1896 and seen here before
amalgamation in Carlisle Citadel station. It
was withdrawn in 1931, and none of the class
members were saved.

► CR 4-6-0 914, Class 908

Here we have a locomotive designed by John F.
McIntosh for the CR. It was built in St Rollox
Works and went into service in December
1906. It is seen light engine in Annan station
yard. On amalgamation, it received the number
14615 and was withdrawn in November 1931.

▲ **CR 4-6-0 907, Class 903**

Here we have another locomotive designed by John F. McIntosh for the CR. It was built in St Rollox Works and went into service in December 1906. It did not reach amalgamation but is included here for interest. This locomotive was involved in Britain's worst-ever railway accident at Quintinshill, Dumfriesshire, on 22 May 1915. It was hauling a local passenger train when it was involved in a double collision and fire involving five trains. At least 226 people were killed; the overwhelming number had been on a troop train and were from the Royal Scots Regiment. The locomotive was taken to St Rollox Works but was found to be beyond repair, and 907 was withdrawn and scrapped. It was the only member of the class of seven not to reach amalgamation, being withdrawn in 1915.

► FR 4-4-0 37, Class K2

A locomotive designed by Robert Harben Whitelegg and built by Sharp, Stewart & Co. for the FR. The engine went into service in 1896 with the number FR 37; on amalgamation, it became part of the LMS with the number 10136. It is seen here at Carnforth shed on 7 July 1923, still bearing the number FR 37. It was withdrawn and condemned in December 1931.

▼ HR 4-6-0 106, Class I

Another Jones-designed locomotive, built in 1894 for the HR by Sharp, Stewart & Co. It went into service in September with the number 106 but was issued with the number 17919 when in the LMS. It is seen here on 29 July 1931 at Killiecrankie station with the 12.20 p.m. train from Perth to Blair Atholl, with one lady waiting to board. It was withdrawn in December 1934.

▲ HR 4-4-0 86, Class L, better known as 'Skye Bogies'

Another Jones-designed class. It was built at Inverness Lochgorm Works for
the HR, going into service in March 1893 with the number 86. It is seen here
at the picturesque Kyle of Lochalsh on 20 June 1927 bearing its LMS number
14279. It was condemned in June 1930.

► HR 4-4-0 92 *Strathdearn*, Class Strath

Designed by David Jones and built by Neilson, Reid &
Co. for the HR. Initially, the number was 92 when first
out of the workshops in June 1892. In 1921 it became
92A, and when taken into the LMS in 1924 it was given
the number 14272. The locomotive is seen here on
16 May 1928, shunting at Forres shed in Scotland. It was
withdrawn from service in June 1930.

◄ CR 4-4-0 186, Class 179

Designed by the CR's locomotive
superintendent, George Brittain, and built at
Dubs & Co. in 1882 as 186. The locomotive
received the number 1186 in 1914. Then,
when coming under the authority of the LMS,
the number 14105 was applied. It is seen here
at Forfar shed in 1930, just before withdrawal
later in that year.

◄ NSR 0-4-4T 19, Class 15

The date is the 13 May 1933, and the location is North Rode, on the Macclesfield to Leek local line. The locomotive is a member of Class 15, built for the NSR. It was constructed at Stoke Railway Works and was designed by John Henry Adams, the locomotive, carriage and wagon superintendent at Stoke. It went into service in 1920, just before the dawn of amalgamation. Its first number was 19, carried from 1920 to 1924, when its LMS number 1438 was affixed. It was withdrawn in January 1936.

► LNWR 4-6-0 5996, Class Claughton

An interesting locomotive is seen at Rowsley in Derbyshire hauling the Royal Train on 3 July 1933 when rebuilt and virtually new. It was originally built in 1912 as a Claughton-Class locomotive with the number 5996, which it carries here. It was rebuilt by the LMS in April 1933 at Derby Works using the old Claughton boilers, wheels and a type of Royal Scot chassis. It then became a member of the Patriot Class and, in 1934, received the number 5528. In 1946, under the LMS, it was again rebuilt by George Ivatt with a large Stanier 2A taper boiler, new cylinders and a double chimney. Like other rebuilt class members, it then resembled a member of the Royal Scot Class. On being inducted into BR, it was given the number 45528, and it went into service unnamed and remained so until September 1959. At this time, it was named *R.E.M.E.* and was later withdrawn on 19 January 1963. It was scrapped at Crewe Works two months later. None of the class members were preserved, but a full-size replica with the number 45551 and the name *Unknown Warrior* is under construction. A model of the locomotive has been made to OO scale by Mainline Models.

► FR 4-4-0 130, Class K4

Seen here at Grange-over-Sands railway station and designed by William Francis Pettigrew in 1913 for the FR. FR 130 was built by the North British Locomotive Company, Glasgow. It held the number FR 130 until being inducted into the LMS, at which time it received the number 10185. It was withdrawn in August 1932 and later scrapped.

◄ LNWR 4-6-0 2122, Class Claughton

Still in LNWR livery at Stalybridge station, Charles Bowen Cooke designed it for the LNWR in September 1917. It was built at Crewe Works and was a powerful locomotive. When taken into the LMS, it was given the number 5956. It was withdrawn in March 1934 and scrapped soon after.

▲ **G&SWR 4-6-4T 545, Class 540**

Photographed outside Glasgow St Enoch station with its LMS number, 15405, this tank engine was designed by Robert Harben Whitelegg and built for the G&SWR by the North British Locomotive Company. Its days on the G&SWR were limited as it was built in April 1922 and was almost immediately entered onto the LMS books. It was withdrawn in August 1936.

◄ **G&SWR 2-6-0 410, Class 403**

Looking scruffy with its active life drawing to a close, No. 410 is at Ayr shed on 5 August 1936, just months before withdrawal. It was built for the G&SWR in 1915, having been designed by Dugald Drummond and built at the North British Locomotive Company, Glasgow. Two months later, it was renumbered 61; in 1919, it was renumbered 54. In 1924 it joined the LMS with the number 17823. It was withdrawn in December 1936.

► **G&SWR 0-6-0 48, Class 17**

It is 1926 and No. 17518 shunts a train of cattle wagons at the goods yard at Annan station, Scotland. The locomotive was designed by James Manson in September 1910 and built at the North British Locomotive Company in Glasgow. It was given firstly the number 48, then in 1919 No. 96. In 1924 the LMS number was 17518; it was withdrawn in 1930.

▼ **L&YR 4-4-2 711, Class 1400**

Hauling a train at Middleton Junction in 1921 is L&YR locomotive No. 711. It was designed by Sir John Audley Frederick Aspinall and built at Horwich Works near Bolton. These were works that the L&YR had built, the company having moved from its original site in Miles Platting in Manchester. In September 1899, it left the works with the number 711. On entering the LMS, this was changed to 10316, and it was withdrawn in March 1934.

▲ **L&YR 0-4-0T 2, Railmotor**

The L&YR employed twenty railmotors in two classes. The Bristol Carriage
and Wagon Company built this one of three in Lot 63. L&YR No. 2 entered
service on 17 December 1909 and, when drawn into the LMS, it received the
number 10614. Railmotors had a steam driving compartment at the front and a
passenger carriage to the rear. No. 10614 is seen here at Stainland and Hollywell
Green station, West Yorkshire, in August 1929. It was withdrawn in June 1937.

▼ **L&YR 2-4-2T 1388, Class 1008**

Seen at Lightcliffe station in West Yorkshire in 1937 is this ancient locomotive designed by Sir John Aspinall and built at Horwich Works in July 1898. When brought into the LMS, it was given the number 10804 and worked through to the next amalgamation in 1949. It then became a member of BR for a very short time. The BR number 50804 was never carried, however, as it was withdrawn in February 1950.

► L&YR 4-6-0 1671, Class 5P

Designed by George Hughes and seen here at Southport Chapel Street station in June 1939 is a locomotive built for the L&YR at Horwich Works that entered service in May 1923 numbered 1671. It went to the LMS the following year with the number 10442. It was another engine that saw the dawn of BR and was allocated the BR number 50442, but it was never fitted. The locomotive was withdrawn in August 1950.

◄ NLR 0-6-0T 27514, Class 2F

This locomotive was built at Bow Works to a design of J.C. Park for the North London Railway (NLR). It was one of a class of thirty locomotives built between 1879 and 1905. They were small but powerful engines constructed to work the docks in London. This one is seen at the Devons Road, Bow shed in 1946. The LNWR also operated them and, on amalgamation, this example was taken into the LMS with the number shown. Before this, the class had two- and three-digit numbers.

At New Mills Newtown station, Derbyshire, in 1934, is a four-cylinder compound locomotive designed by Francis Webb and built at Crewe Works in May 1904. On amalgamation, it joined the LMS, and in 1927 it was renumbered 9357. In 1948, when joining BR, the number was changed to 49357. It was allocated to Carnforth and withdrawn on 14 October 1961. It was scrapped at Cashmore's of Great Bridge. The locomotives of this class were known as 'Super Ds'.

► MR 0-10-0 2290, Class Big Bertha

This unique locomotive was built by the MR, going into service in December 1919 as 2290. Henry Fowler designed it as a one-off to perform banking on the Lickey Incline, and it was built at Derby Works. The one-off class was Big Bertha; as the First World War had just ended, that name could have been taken from the well-known name of a big German field gun. It came to describe something large or cumbersome, especially in respect of machinery. It is seen here doing its duty as a banker on the Lickey Incline near Bromsgrove; the date is 26 April 1932, by which time it was part of the LMS and its number had changed to 22290. On 29 January 1949, it became part of BR with the number 58100. On Saturday, 19 May 1956, it was withdrawn from service and taken back to Derby Works for scrapping. There ends the long life of the only locomotive of its kind in the world. The light from the front was transferred to the engine that was to take over the Lickey duties, 9F 2-10-0 92079. This engine was itself scrapped at Campbells of Airdrie in April 1968.

▼ MR 4-2-2 97, Class 1853

Seen here at Tamworth with a long passenger train on 27 June 1925 is a double-header with ex-MR 644 piloting MR 498. MR 644 was a member of one of four locomotive classes known as 'Spinners' due to the one large single-driving wheel in the centre of the 4-2-2-wheel arrangement and their excellent turn of speed. It was built at Derby Works in March 1892 with the number 97, being renumbered 644 in 1907. It had just one year to go when the photo was taken, never receiving a BR number. It was withdrawn for scrapping in April 1926. The train locomotive MR 498 was built at Derby Works in November 1897 and was later modified by Henry Fowler and fitted with superheaters. It had a far longer lifespan than its pilot, receiving the BR number 40498 in 1948. It was not withdrawn until Saturday, 26 August 1950 and scrapped in October of the same year at Derby Works. Samuel Waite Johnson designed both locomotives.

▲ MR 4-4-0 1019, Class 4P

Another Johnson-designed locomotive, it was built at Derby Works in 1919 for the MR in anticipation of joining the LMS. It is seen here near Ambergate in April 1927 hauling a passenger train. Spending most of its life within the LMS, it reached nationalisation in 1948 and received the BR number 41019. It was withdrawn on 17 April 1951 and scrapped in March 1952 at Derby.

▲ **MR 0-6-0 3882, Class 4F**

Henry Fowler, later Sir, was the CME with the MR and later held the same position in the LMS. He was the designer of the large Class-4F goods engines, known in enthusiast circles as 'Duck Sixes' due to their wheel arrangement. This 4F was built at Derby Works in 1919 for the MR/LMS. A total of 575 4F locomotives were built between seven railway works. In this photograph, 3882 is passing Norman's Bank at Hope Valley, Derbyshire, on 7 August 1937, with an unfitted freight. Another locomotive with a long life of hard work, it received the BR number 43882 on 7 May 1949. It was withdrawn on 29 June 1963 for scrapping in July that year.

▲ MR 0-6-0 3842, Class 4F

Another Fowler-designed engine for the MR/LMS, No. 3842
was built at Derby Works in 1917. It is seen here with a mineral
train passing over King's Norton level crossing, Birmingham, on
11 March 1922. The locomotive could be found at Buxton shed on
1 January 1948, and on 6 November, it was renumbered 43842.
It was withdrawn from BR Buxton on 28 November 1959 and
scrapped in March 1960 by T.W. Ward Ltd of Killamarsh.

◄ MR 0-4-4T 1211, Class 690

This ancient locomotive is a well tank with the tank beneath the bunker (a double frame). They were designed by Matthew Kirtley and manufactured by Beyer, Peacock & Co. in 1869 for the MR. The class consisted of just six 0-4-4T locomotives built specifically for coal traffic on the widened lines to Herne Hill and Battersea. On amalgamation with the LMS, it received the number 1211. The class had all been scrapped by August 1934. This example is at St Pancras station in September 1932 with, presumably, the guard relaxing on the van behind the engine, while the fireman or driver looks back towards him.

► MR 4-4-0 1024, Class 4P

Designed by S.W. Johnson for MR, 1024 was built at Derby Works and entered service in June 1906. No. 1024 is seen here at Gloucester on 15 May 1933, with a passenger train; the first coach is the clerestory type. The locomotive was in service up to nationalisation. It was issued with the BR number 41024 but never received it, being withdrawn on 2 October 1948 from Sheffield Millhouses, and scrapped in the same year at Derby Works. One famous class sister was preserved with the number 1000 and can be seen at the National Railway Museum, York, when not on loan to Barrow Hill Roundhouse or out on the metals.

Locomotives Built by the London, Midland and Scottish Railway

▲ LMS 4-6-0 14637, Class 60

A locomotive built by the new LMS within the Big Four in Edinburgh Princes Street station. It was designed by W. Pickersgill and built at St Rollox Works, Glasgow, in 1924, going into service in July 1926. It was allocated to Motherwell Motive Power Depot (MPD). While based at Motherwell in 1948, it was given a BR number, 54637, but it was never fitted as the engine was withdrawn two months later and scrapped at Kilmarnock Works soon after.

▲ LMS 4-6-2 6207 *Princess Arthur of Connaught*, Class Princess Royal

Crewe North yard gives us a publicity photo of the new Princess Royal-Class 6207 *Princess Arthur of Connaught*; the photo was taken on 18 August 1935. The locomotive had gone into service on 9 August 1935. It had a starring role when its building was recorded to make the classic 1930s documentary *No 6207, A Study in Steel*. The film featured the construction of a railway engine from molten metal to a completed locomotive. On nationalisation, the engine received the number 46207.

Sadly, this locomotive was involved in two crashes.

The engine was hauling the Glasgow to London Euston express on 17 April 1946; it had stopped just outside Winsford in Cheshire after the communication cord was pulled. The person responsible was a soldier coming on leave who did, in fact, work as a signal-box lad at Winsford but was doing his National Service, so he thought that he was safe and that the train would stop before the points. He had got it wrong; the following postal express hauled by No. 46251 *City of Nottingham* ran into the stopped train at about 40–45mph. Twenty-four passengers were killed and ten injured. The error was with the Winsford signalman who reported the line clear and had given the postal the all clear. The soldier gave himself up and retained his job in the signal box, not retiring until the 1990s. This was the first significant accident after nationalisation.

On Friday, 21 September 1951, 46207 was hauling the 08.20 Liverpool to London service comprising fifteen coaches. Just south of Weedon in Northamptonshire, the engine began to derail while travelling at 65mph. The inevitable crash killed fifteen people and injured thirty-five more. The cause of the accident was that the engine had just had its wheelsets moved around, and one of the bogie axle boxes was too tight, causing a jammed axle box. The engine was taken to Crewe Works for repair. It entered the works on 23 September 1951 and departed back into service on 22 December. It was withdrawn on 25 November 1961 and scrapped at Crewe Works in May 1962.

▶ LMS 4-6-2 6202 'Turbomotive'

Seen at Crewe Works in 1935, its year of manufacture, is a unique experimental locomotive designed by Stanier and based on the Princess Royal Class with a tapered boiler. It used turbines instead of cylinders and was relatively successful in cutting down the amount of coal required and caused less damage to the track, being smoother. However, it was not perfect, and when there was a turbine failure in 1949, it was decided that it was not economical to continue with the project. Instead, in 1952, it was rebuilt as a conventional locomotive in the Princess Class. By this time, BR had taken over, and the new engine was numbered 46202 and named *Princess Anne*.

On 8 October 1952, it had only been in service for two months when it was involved in the second-worst peacetime train crash ever. It was the lead engine, double-headed with 45637 *Windward Islands*, on the London to Manchester and Liverpool express. A local train was standing at the platform in Harrow and Wealdstone station during the morning rush hour. An overnight express from Perth hauled by 46242 *City of Glasgow* smashed into the rear of the local train, spreading wreckage across all lines and platforms. Within seconds the Liverpool to Manchester express travelling north slammed into the wreckage. The investigation found that the Perth train driver had missed a caution signal and two danger signals before colliding with the stopped local train. A total of 112 people were killed and 340 injured. The only crash with more fatalities was the Quintinshill rail disaster in 1915, when 226 people died.

The locomotive 46202 was beyond repair and was taken back to Crewe Works, withdrawn on 2 May 1954, and scrapped there.

▶ LMS 4-6-0 5152, Class 5MT

The first of our more modern Big Four members is this Stanier-designed Black Five, seen here at Ayr station in 1937. The locomotive was one of the earlier members of an extensive class of superb engines designed by Stanier. It was built by Armstrong Whitworth and went into service in June 1935 for the LMS. At this time, it was allocated to Carlisle Kingmoor, and its last shed was Motherwell. On entering BR, the number was changed to 45152. It was withdrawn on 31 December 1962 and scrapped at Motherwell Machinery and Scrap, Inslow Works, Wishaw.

◄ **LMS 4-6-0 5507 *Royal Tank Corps*, Class Patriot**

No. 5507 at Edge Hill shed in Liverpool shortly after being built at Crewe Works on 12 August 1932. It was named the *Royal Tank Corps* before the first allocation. The designer was Henry Fowler, and unlike many of this large class, it was not rebuilt to the design of Stanier. It was brought into BR on amalgamation, and the number was changed to 45507. The locomotive was scrapped on 23 March 1963.

► **LMS 4-6-0 6149 *Lady of the Lake*, Class Royal Scot**

This Royal Scot locomotive is hauling a theatrical tour train as it passes over Hademore Troughs at Lichfield on 12 March 1933. The engine was built by the North British Locomotive Company in Glasgow and introduced in December 1927 to Sir Henry Fowler's design. It was first named *Lady of the Lake* on introduction and in May 1936 was renamed *Middlesex Regiment*. In 1945 it was rebuilt to a Stanier tapered boiler design and later fitted with windshields. On 31 August 1963, it was withdrawn and broken up at Crewe Works four months later.

► LMS 4-6-0 6101 *Royal Scots Grey*, Class Royal Scot

Stopping to pick up passengers at Tebay station on 28 July 1947 is Fowler-designed Royal Scot *Royal Scots Grey*. It was built at the North British Locomotive Company in Glasgow and introduced on 11 September 1927. In November 1945, it was rebuilt to a Stanier design with a taper boiler and later windshields. On amalgamation in 1949, it received the BR number 46101; then, on 30 April 1962, it was the second member of the class to have its nameplates removed. And in this case, they were affixed to 'Deltic' locomotive D9000, which became *Royal Scots Grey*. In September 1963, 46101 was condemned and scrapped the following year at Slag Reduction Co. Ltd, Ickles, Rotherham.

◄ LMS 4-6-0 6005, Class Patriot

Passing through the cutting at Whitmore, an area used for speed trials, is Patriot engine 5509 with a short train of milk tanks. The locomotive was designed by Fowler and built at Crewe Works, being introduced on 19 August 1932. The LMS number was originally 6005, later 5509, and 45509 on going into BR. Then, in 1951, it received its name, *The Derbyshire Yeomanry*. It was withdrawn in August 1961 and scrapped at Crewe Works on 30 September that year. It has been replicated as a OO scale model by Steamline Ltd.

◄ LMS 4-6-0 6008 *Lady Godiva*, Class Patriot

The locomotive *Lady Godiva*, 5519, is seen here at Crewe Works in 1936. This Fowler-designed locomotive was built at Crewe Works, being released on 22 February 1933, having been rebuilt from an LNWR Claughton. Its pre-1935 number was 6008 and then 5519, followed by 45519 on entering BR and with the class nicknamed 'Baby Scots'. None were preserved and, accordingly, at least one is now being built with the name *Unknown Warrior*. Eighteen of the class were Stanier rebuilds; this was not one of them. This rebuild was a paper exercise as all were virtually new locomotives. No. 45519 was withdrawn on 17 March 1962 and scrapped at Crewe Works almost immediately. Hornby built a OO scale model of this locomotive.

▼ LMS 4-6-0 5568 *Western Australia*, Class Jubilee

No. 5568 is in first-class condition on the Crewe station platform in 1946. It was designed by Stanier and built by the North British Locomotive Company in Glasgow, going into service on 25 August 1934. In 1936 it received the name *Western Australia*. It is seen paired with a Fowler tender.

On 21 January 1938, this locomotive was involved in a serious accident at Oakley Junction in Bedfordshire. A train of empty stock arrived at the junction to stable the stock on the way and works sidings. There followed a swathe of human error, leaving the train of empty stock fouling the main line. The St Pancras to Bradford express, hauled by 5568 *Western Australia*, was approaching at 75mph. The driver, H.J. Hudson, saw a distant signal at caution and applied the brakes to slow the train, but by the time he saw the next signal at danger and applied the brakes fully, he could not drop below 25mph. The engines collided, and the Bradford train's carriages were thrown around, causing three fatalities, one of whom was driver Hudson, and eight injured; the driver of the other engine suffered a broken leg. On amalgamation, 5568 became 45568. It was withdrawn on 25 April 1964 and scrapped at Drapers of Neptune St Goods Yard, Hull.

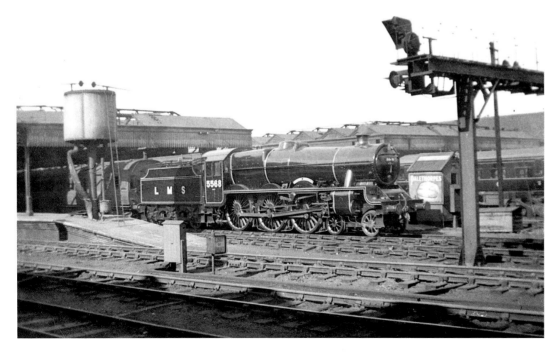

▲ LMS 4-6-0 6100 *Kings Dragoon Guardsman*, Class Royal Scot

In 1930, the locomotive originally named the *Kings Dragoon Guardsman* was first allocated at Camden after construction at Derby Works. It went into service in June 1930 and in December 1933 it was renamed *Royal Scot*, and this is the name displayed throughout its service life and preservation. On becoming part of BR, the number was altered to 46100.

The original 6100 was built by the North British Locomotive Company in Glasgow and named *Royal Scot*. In 1933 the locomotives exchanged numbers, and the *Kings Dragoon Guardsman* became the *Royal Scot*.

This was before it was exhibited at the Century of Progress Exhibition. It then toured the US and Canada by the then-named *Royal Scot* and a rake of LMS carriages. It was partially stripped down and loaded onto the Canadian Pacific ship SS *Beaverdale*. After touring the two countries, it was awarded a plaque, which is displayed beneath the *Royal Scot* name.

On 13 October 1962, the *Royal Scot* was withdrawn and condemned, but that was not the end. Billy Butlin purchased it for his holiday camp in Skegness,

and it was withdrawn for cosmetic upgrade and painted in Crimson Lake at Crewe Works It was then hauled to Ingoldmells and the Butlin's camp, where it arrived on 18 July 1963 and was welcomed by pipers from the Royal Scots. It was then displayed on a plinth. Only two class members were saved in this way; the other one was 6115 *Scots Guardsman*.

On 16 March 1971, *Royal Scot* departed Butlin's for the Bressingham Steam Museum and the following year it returned to steam and worked until 1978. It then became a static exhibition again until Billy Butlin, now a Sir, sold it to the Bressingham Museum. It was sold to the Royal Scot Locomotive and General Trust in April 2009, at which time it was moved to Peter Waterman's LNW Heritage workshops in Crewe. On the way to a steam gala at the West Somerset Railway on a low-loader, the lorry caught fire on the M5, causing some damage to the locomotive. It was withdrawn to await a complete overhaul to main-line standard, and on completion its first railtour took place on Saturday, 6 February 2016.

◀ **LMS 4-6-0 5529** *Sir Herbert Walker KCB*, **Class Patriot**

No. 5529 was rebuilt by Henry Fowler at Crewe Works from an ex-LNWR Claughton design, going into service on 6 April 1933. It received its first name in 1938. In 1948 it was rebuilt to a design by Stanier, replacing the parallel boiler with a large taper boiler, also with a double chimney and new cylinders. Seen at Lichfield station on 7 April 1939, it is without a name, but until 1937 it had been called *Sir Herbert Walker KCB*, an identity that was then transferred to 45535 in this year. A backing plate for a name remained blank until the rebuild by BR in 1948. It then received the name *Stephenson* to commemorate the centenary of George Stephenson's death; it was also renumbered 45529 at this time. It was withdrawn on 22 February 1964 and scrapped at Crewe Works six days later.

▶ **LMS 4-6-0 6117** *Welsh Guardsman*, **Class Royal Scot**

A young enthusiast peers from behind a lamp standard as 6117 *Welsh Guardsman* thunders through Prestatyn station with the down Irish Mail on 14 May 1936. The locomotive was designed by Henry Fowler and built at the North British Locomotive Company in November 1927. It was rebuilt in 1944 with a Stanier taper boiler, a double chimney and new cylinders. On nationalisation, it received the number 46117, and on 18 April 1952 it was double-headed hauling the up Thames Clyde express when involved in an accident on Blea Moor Loops. There was a defect on the other locomotive acting as pilot, an old compound 41040, that caused a set of points to move under the train when they were struck by a brake lever that had dropped and been dragging for 2 miles. No. 46117 was thrown onto its side, and thirty-four passengers were injured, but fortunately there were no fatalities. Several companies have modelled *Welsh Guardsman* in OO scale.

► **LMS 4-6-0 6170** *British Legion*, **Class Royal Scot**

Seen at Crewe North shed on 14 September 1937 is a relatively new locomotive, two years old at that time. In 1929 the search was on for a cheaper way to run steam traction, and one idea was to use of high-pressure steam. To this end, the North British Locomotive Company built a steam locomotive to experiment with superpower steam. Similar experiments were going on around the world at the time. The engine was authorised by Henry Fowler, the LMS CME, and built in conjunction with the LMS and the Superheater Company.

The experimental engine was given the number 6399 and the name *Fury*. It had a long, complex boiler built by the Superheater Company and a complicated three-stage, Schmidt-based boiler. The engine was technically an ultra-high-pressure steam compound locomotive. On a test trip on 10 February 1930, one of the boiler tubes burst, firing high-pressure steam and the firebox's contents into the cab and instantly killing a Superheater Company member. Many tests were carried out and the engine was rebuilt, but things did not go to plan, and the engine did not run until 1933. In 1935 the locomotive was rebuilt at Crewe Works under Stanier. A more conventional boiler was used, and the locomotive joined the traditional Royal Scot Class with the number 6170, *British Legion*. At the time, Stanier had more on his mind as he was working on another ill-fated locomotive, 'Turbomotive'.

No. 6170 was rebuilt with a Stanier taper boiler and was the only Royal Scot in service to be painted in Crimson Lake red and sport a single chimney, although it later received a double chimney and windshields. On nationalisation, it was renumbered 56170. It was withdrawn on 1 December 1962 and scrapped at Crewe Works.

► **LMS 4-6-0 6118** *Royal Welch Fusilier*, **Class Royal Scot**

Seen on 11 September 1948 as it passes through Crewe station is Royal Scot 6118 *Royal Welch Fusilier*. Soon, nationalisation will arrive, and a four will be added to its number, making it 46118. The locomotive was designed by Fowler and built at the North British Locomotive Company in Glasgow, going into service in November 1927. In December 1946, it was rebuilt by Stanier with a tapered boiler and later had windshields fitted. It was withdrawn on 13 June 1964 and scrapped at J.N. Connell's scrapyard, Coatbridge.

► **LMS 4-6-0 6137 *Vesta*, Class Royal Scot**

Seen near Carlisle Citadel station with an up express in the 1930s is an unrebuilt Royal Scot. The locomotive was designed by Henry Fowler and built at the North British Locomotive Company in Glasgow. It was initially named *Vesta* and went into service on 9 October 1927. Under BR, as 46137, it was rebuilt by Stanier at Crewe Works in March 1955 with a taper boiler, as the last of the Royal Scot Class to undergo the work. It was withdrawn on 3 November 1962 and scrapped at Crewe Works on 9 May 1963.

◄ **LMS 4-6-2 6200 *Princess Royal*, Class Princess Royal**

Photographed at Crewe Works on 27 August 1935 is 6200 *Princess Royal*. It was named after the Princess Royal at the time, Princess Mary, Countess of Harewood. The locomotive was just two years old, having been built at Crewe Works, going into service on 27 June 1933. The designer was Stanier, with his taper boiler feature. When photographed, it had just finished in the works after nine days, which was followed in November by a sixty-seven-day refit. The locomotive was the first of the class to be built, on 27 July 1933. It was then the last to be withdrawn, on 17 November 1962, and was scrapped at Connell's scrapyard. Only two of the eleven class members were preserved.

▲ LMS 4-6-2 6220 *Coronation*, Class Coronation

Here we have another class leader in 6220 *Coronation*, seen at Brinklow station in 1937. The locomotive was designed by Stanier and built at Crewe Works in June 1937. It was not painted conventionally in red but with CR blue. This colour scheme was used on later class members. As covered in our book *Remembering Steam*, this locomotive broke the world speed record for a steam engine. This new locomotive travelled at 114mph on Madeley Bank, beating the LNER, which held the 113mph record. The crew, including Robert Riddles, were so excited that they nearly overran the Crewe station points. This close call stopped further competitions, and it was a year before *Mallard*, 'testing its brakes', reached 126mph on Stoke Bank, a record that still stands. *Coronation* temporarily swapped numbers with 6229 *Duchess of Hamilton*, and that

locomotive toured the US with the name and number of *Coronation*. This left a red 6220 touring the US for the World Fair and a blue 5229 in the UK! The numbers and names were returned to the correct engines on return.

At nationalisation, *Coronation* received the number 46220 in 1948; simultaneously, it was fitted with a double chimney and the streamlining was removed. It was equipped with smoke deflectors at the same time, and its condition then gave it the name 'semi' for semi-streamlined. It was later painted BR green and had a sloping smokebox from the previous streamlining until 1957, when a conventional one was fitted.

Coronation was the first of the class to be withdrawn, on 30 April 1963. It was scrapped on 30 May that year at Crewe Works.

▲ **LMS 4-6-0 5688** *Polyphemus*, **Class Jubilee**

The war has just about ended, it is 1945, and two trainspotters are at the
southern end of Crewe station. They are getting ready to record the oncoming
engine in their Ian Allan ABC guides and have already recognised it as a
'Jub'. No. 5688 *Polyphemus* will soon have a line under it in their books.
The locomotive, designed by Stanier, was built at Crewe Works, going into
service on 23 February 1936. It was one of just 191 locomotives in the class
constructed between 1934 and 1936. These trainspotters probably knew them
as Red Staniers after the colour when new. *Polyphemus* was withdrawn on
15 December 1962 and scrapped on 13 June 1963 at Crewe Works.

▲ LMS 4-6-0 5589 *Gwalior*, Class Jubilee

Hest Bank, Lancaster, in 1937, sees Jubilee 5589 *Gwalior* passing
with a long train of maroon carriages. The Stanier locomotive was
built at the North British Locomotive Company in Glasgow and
went into service on 15 December 1934. On nationalisation, it
acquired the number 45589 and was withdrawn on 26 March 1965
to be broken up a year later at Cashmore's of Great Bridge.

◀ LMS 4-6-2 6200 *Princess Royal*, Class Princess Royal

It is June 1933, and a member of the Princess Royal Class, 6200, is under construction in Crewe Works. It will enter BR in August 1948 with the number 46200. The class provided traction for the non-stop Coronation Scot expresses, and these beautiful locomotives were used on goods trains towards the end of their service. The electrification of the West Coast Main Line (WCML) prohibited them from travelling under the wires. Then, dieselisation was introduced in the early 1960s, and the whole class became surplus to requirements. *Princess Royal* was withdrawn from Carlisle Kingmoor shed on Saturday, 17 November 1962 and scrapped at J.N. Connell's scrapyard in October 1964.

◀ LMS 4-6-2 6208 *Princess Helena Victoria*, Class Princess Royal

On the WCML sits little Acton Bridge station, and here passing through in 1946 with an up express is 6208 *Princess Helena Victoria*. The Stanier locomotive was built in August 1935 at Crewe Works. On nationalisation, the number was amended to 46208. It was withdrawn on Saturday, 10 October 1962 from Edge Hill and scrapped two months later at Crewe Works.

◄ LMS 4-6-0 5536 *Private W. Wood VC*, Class Patriot

Macclesfield Central is the location of 5536 *Private W. Wood VC* on 21 September 1938. It was designed by Henry Fowler and built at Crewe Works, going into service on 4 May 1933, at which time it was unnamed. In 1936 it was named and unveiled by Private Wilfrid Wood, who was awarded the Victoria Cross in the First World War. After the war, Wilfrid returned to his job on the railways, firstly as a fireman and then driver. He retired in 1960 with the position of supervisor.

On nationalisation, the locomotive received the number 45536. It was rebuilt by Ivatt in 1946, giving it a taper boiler and double chimney. The engine was withdrawn on 29 December 1962 and scrapped in March 1964. The locomotive is now a OO scale model made by Hornby Ltd, and a nameplate is displayed at Norbury Hall primary school in Manchester, where the war hero had been a pupil.

◄ LMS 4-6-2 6243 *City of Lancaster*, Class Coronation

Still in its wartime livery, 6243 is seen entering Tebay station with a passenger train on 27 August 1947. It was designed by Stanier and built at Crewe Works in June 1940 in streamlined form. In 1946 all the streamlined class members started to have it removed. In April 1948, it was renumbered 46243, but the streamlining was not removed until May 1949, when windshields were fitted and it became a semi. This meant that it became the only locomotive in the class to be streamlined during nationalisation, if only for a very short while. Simultaneously, it became the first of two class members to be painted blue, but only until 1955, when maroon paint was applied to sixteen class members. It was withdrawn in October 1964, and after an attempt to get it preserved, it was scrapped in August 1965 at the Central Wagon Co., Ince, Wigan.

► LMS 0-4-0T 7191, Class Sentinel

This unusual locomotive was released in September 1929 for the LMS. It was built by the Sentinel Waggon Works, possibly better known for its road vehicles. The locomotive went into service with the Somerset and Dorset Railway (SDJR) the same month at Bath Green Park as a shunting engine. It is seen here at Derby shed on 15 October 1933. In May 1952 it was taken into BR on nationalisation and given the number 47191. On 25 August 1959, it was condemned, withdrawn and scrapped at Crewe Works the same year.

◄ LMS 2-6-0 0-6-2 4978, Class Garratt

A quite unusual sight on BR was the Beyer Garratt locomotive, and here we have one near Howden in Yorkshire on 30 March 1933. They were designed by Henry Fowler and Beyer Garratt, with the building supervised by Ivatt, and built for the LMS by Beyer, Peacock & Co., going into service in September 1930. In 1938 it was renumbered 7978, and then in November 1948 received the BR number 47978. The small class was built for heavy goods work. No. 47978 was withdrawn on 16 March 1957 and scrapped at Crewe Works a month later.

▲ LMS Co-Co 10000, Class D16/1

One of two experimental diesel locomotives, No. 10000 is seen here at St Pancras station in 1948. They were designed and built in conjunction with English Electric and Derby Works for the LMS. Its sister was 10001, and they were the first main-line diesel locomotives built in Britain. This one went into service at Camden on 30 November 1947. It was completed just four weeks before nationalisation and had the LMS logo; 10001 was outshopped in July 1948, so accordingly went straight into BR with the BR logo. No. 10000 carried the LMS logo until 1951 simply because Ivatt kept 'losing' the paperwork. When he retired, the BR logo was quickly appended.

Both locomotives were well tested on various train types, including the Royal Scot, and performed well both singly and double-headed. They were found to be suitable and singly on a par with a Black Five; double-headed, they compared well with a Standard-Class 7. No. 10000 was withdrawn in December 1963 and was then retained as a donor for its sister engine 10001, which remained in service until 1966. Attempts were made to preserve 10000 and it was offered to the Clapham Rail Museum, but it declined as there was no room! No. 10000 was scrapped at Cashmore's of Great Bridge in January 1968. In 2011 the Ivatt Diesel Re-creation Society announced that they planned to build a replica of 10000. As a young enthusiast, I was delighted to see lots of steam locomotives. That notwithstanding, my sensible head struggled to see why, with such successful diesel prototypes with so much potential, steam engines were still built until the 1960s.

▲ **LMS 4-6-2 6226 *Duchess of Norfolk*, Class Coronation**

LMS Coronation 6226 *Duchess of Norfolk* steams quietly at Crewe station in 1938. The Stanier-designed engine was built at Crewe Works in September 1938 at the cost of £11,302. On nationalisation, it was taken into BR and had a four added to the number, making it 46226. This locomotive class was the most powerful in Britain and designed explicitly for express work on the WCML. It was streamlined but would lose this in 1948 or 1949 and be fitted with windshields, but still with a sloping front to the smokebox. No. 6226 was the first of the class to receive a cylindrical smokebox in 1952. In 1964 work was under way to electrify the WCML, and the class was too high to pass under the wires safely. Initially, they had a yellow stripe down the sides to indicate that they should not travel south of Crewe. It led to them being withdrawn somewhat prematurely. The *Duchess of Norfolk* was withdrawn in September 1964 and scrapped the following month at Arnott, Young & Co. in Troon.

► LMS Diesel Multiple Units
80000, 80001, 80002

This was a diesel multiple unit seen at Oxford in 1938. The LMS planned to produce a more up-to-date and comfortable set. What they decided upon was a three-car set of articulated railcars. Stanier had already developed articulated carriages for locomotive-hauled stock, so there was a precedent. The Derby Carriage and Wagon Works built the units in 1939 for the LMS and they were numbered 80000, 80001 and 80002. They were streamlined and quite attractive, with two Leyland 125bhp diesel engines under each coach. The units first worked the Varsity line between Oxford Rewley Road and Cambridge, followed by the St Pancras to Nottingham service. The set was withdrawn on the outbreak of the Second World War and never used by the public again. In 1949 it was converted into a two-car set with the roofs flattened for overhead line maintenance, and the carriages were for the staff and tools. It was used on the Manchester to Altrincham line, and then in 1959, it was moved to the Longsight Depot and taken out of service. It was still there in a derelict state in 1967.

► LMS 2-8-0 8627, Class 8F

This powerful engine's size is put into perspective as it stands brand new at Brighton Railway Works, with a staff member in the doorway. One of a large class of locomotives designed by Stanier for the LMS, this one was built at Brighton in May 1943 and put straight to work during the Second World War. On 1 May 1948, it was taken into BR with the new number 48627. It was withdrawn on 5 March 1966 from Kirkby in Ashfield and scrapped three months later. The class could be seen on the Imperial Chemical Industries (ICI) traffic in the north-west, and enthusiasts nicknamed them 'Consuls'.

▲ **LMS 4-6-2 6225** *Duchess of Gloucester,* **Class Coronation**

Carlisle Citadel station on a wet day in August 1939 sees the down midday service about to set off with 6225 *Duchess of Gloucester* in charge. The Stanier engine, complete in vibrant streamlined condition, would soon get a coat of black as the war was only a few weeks away. It was built at Crewe Works for £11,302, going into service on 11 May 1938 at Camden MPD. The stream-lining was removed in 1946, giving it the nickname 'semi'. On nationalisation, it carried the BR number 46225 and was withdrawn from Carlisle Upperby on 30 September 1964, being scrapped at Arnott, Young & Co. in Troon the following month. It was built as a model by Bassett-Lowke in both streamlined and semi-streamlined. It is also a OO model made by Hornby.

THE LONDON AND NORTH EASTERN RAILWAY (LNER)

The prominent constituent companies incorporated into the LNER on amalgamation:

North Eastern Railway (NER): 1,757 miles (2,829km)
North British Railway (NBR): 1,378 miles (2,218km)
Great Eastern Railway (GER): 1,191 miles (1,917km)
Great Northern Railway (GNR): 1,051 miles (1,692km)
Great Central Railway (GCR): 852 miles (1,372km)

Great North of Scotland Railway (GNSR): 334 miles (538km)
Hull and Barnsley Railway (H&BR): 106 miles (171km)

Many of these companies had their own subsidiaries. For instance, the Cheshire Lines Committee (CLC) owned their own rolling stock and leased locomotives from the LNER. This was after amalgamation and until nationalisation. There were also many small, independently operated lines of short distances.

Locomotives in Companies Drawn into the London and North Eastern Railway on Amalgamation

◀ GCR 4-4-2 365 *Sir William Pollitt*, Class C5

Inside Gorton Railway Works in Manchester, and we see a locomotive designed by John George Robinson under construction. The date is December 1906, and the shiny new locomotive is GCR No. 365, to be named *Sir William Pollitt*. On 5 September 1925, on becoming part of the LNER, the number was changed to 5365, then on 1 September 1946, it became 2898. It was withdrawn on 25 August 1947 and broken up at Gorton Works. Sir William Pollitt was a railway manager at the Manchester, Sheffield and Lincolnshire Railway (MS&LR), later the GCR.

▲ **GCR 4-2-2 971, Class X4 13**

Seen here at Trafford Park shed in 1922 and in a very smart condition is GCR No. 971. It was designed by Harry Pollitt, the son of the aforenamed Sir William, and built at Gorton Works, going into service in November 1900. It was allocated the LNER number 5971 but was withdrawn in December 1923, never having carried it. The locomotive was scrapped at Gorton Works.

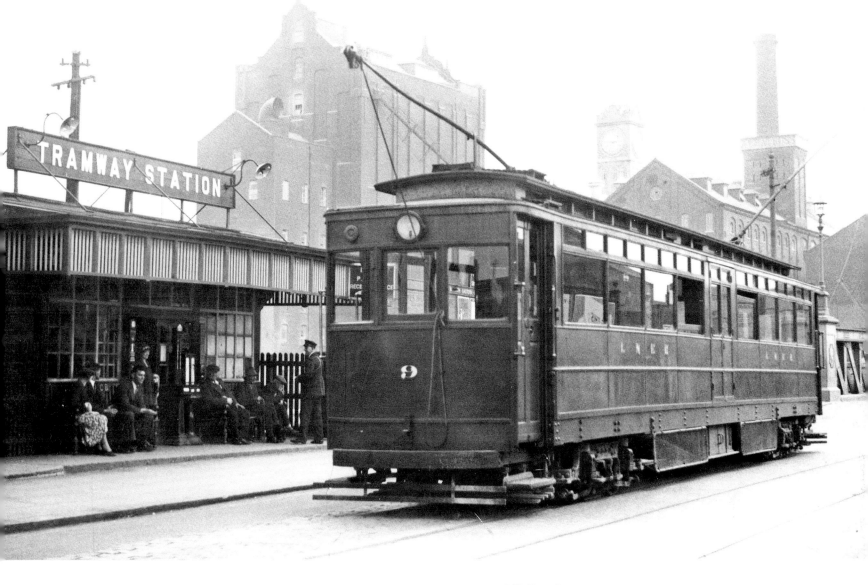

▲ GCR, Tram 9

An unusual view of Tram 9 at the Grimsby Tramway Terminus on 11 July 1937. The Brush company built this one for the GCR in around 1913, and here it has been incorporated into the LNER. Not listed as one of those preserved, the line ran from 1912 until, on 1 July 1961, it was finally closed by BR.

◄ **GNR 2-6-0 1651, Class K2**

Seen here hauling a goods train at New Southgate, a suburb of London, is GNR locomotive 1651. It was designed by Gresley and built at Doncaster Works for the GNR, going into service in February 1916. It was taken into the LNER in 1924 with the number 4651, then in March 1946, 1741. On 11 September 1948, it was given the BR number 61741. It was withdrawn from Kittybrewster, Aberdeen, on 11 March 1960 and cut up at Cowlairs British Rail Works a month later.

► **GER 4-6-0 1520, Class S69**

Seen here at Gorton shed in 1932 is a locomotive designed by Stephen Holden for the GER and released into service from Stratford Works in April 1914 with the number 1520. It was drawn into the LNER on amalgamation and renumbered 8520, as seen here. In August 1927 it was modified with the fitting of a vacuum ejector. Here it will have just been fitted with ACFI feedwater apparatus, which can be seen on the top of the boiler and was removed in January 1940. Under BR in September 1948 it became 61520. The locomotive was withdrawn on Monday, 24 June 1957 and scrapped in September that year.

▲ GCR 4-4-2 1093, Class C4

Cressington in 1935 and LNER 6093 is hauling a 'Grand National Excursion'. Members of the class were nicknamed 'Jersey Lillies' after the actress and friend of the Prince of Wales, Lillie Langtry. This locomotive was designed by Robinson and built at the North British Locomotive Company in Glasgow. It went into service for the GCR in November 1905 with the number 1093. On amalgamation, it joined the LNER in 1924 as 6093, the number it displays here. In 1946 the number was changed by the LNER to 2916. Then, at nationalisation, the number allocated but never carried was 62916. It was withdrawn on 13 November 1948 and scrapped the same month; none of the class locomotives were preserved.

► GCR 4-6-0 1165 *Valour*, Class B3

Here GCR 6165 *Valour* is standing at Nottingham Victoria station in 1928. Designed by Robinson for the GCR and built at Gorton Works in Manchester with the number 1165, the locomotive went into service at Gorton in July 1920. In 1925 it became part of the LNER with the number 6165. On 1 September 1946, it received the LNER number 1496. It was withdrawn at Lincoln on 31 December 1947 and scrapped at the Dukinfield Carriage Works soon after.

◄ GCR 4-4-0 501 *Mons*, Class 11F

Another Robinson-designed locomotive, built at Gorton Works in September 1922 for the GCR with the number 501 and named *Mons* after the First World War battle. Class D11 is the Robinson Class for the GCR and 11F denotes an 'Improved Director'. The locomotive is seen here in 1935 approaching Crowden station on the Woodhead line between Manchester and Sheffield; this line has now gone. In November 1924, the locomotive was taken into the LNER with the number 5501. In May 1946, it received the LNER identity 2665 and then during nationalisation in June 1948 it was renumbered 62665. It was withdrawn in May 1959 and scrapped at Gorton Works two months later.

◀ GNR 2-6-0 1698 *Loch Rannoch*, Class H3

Now in Scotland and on the turntable at Mallaig shed is LNER 4698 *Loch Rannoch*. Gresley designed the locomotive, and Kitson & Co. built it in August 1921 for the GNR. The number was 1698 *Loch Rannoch* until becoming part of the LNER in May 1924, when it was changed to 4698. It went into service in August 1921 at New England, Peterborough, but it spent the rest of its career in Scotland. On 19 April 1948, as a BR engine, it carried the number 61788. It was withdrawn from Eastfield shed on Monday, 26 June 1961 after almost forty years in service. It was broken up at Cowlairs Works six months later.

▶ GNR 4-4-2 1404, Class C1

King's Cross station in 1912 and the relatively new GNR locomotive 1404 stands at the platform; note the period horse-drawn carriage waiting for or dropping off customers. The locomotive was designed by Ivatt and built at Doncaster Works in June 1905. It was released into service in the same month and after nineteen years it became part of the LNER and was given the number 4404. On 14 September 1946, the number was changed to 2834, but it never reached nationalisation, being withdrawn on 8 August 1947 from King's Cross and scrapped at Darlington Locomotive Works shortly after.

◄ GCR 4-4-0 505 *Ypres*, Class D11

Designed by Robinson and built at Gorton Works for the GCR, it was released into service as 505 *Ypres*, named after the First World War battle. When being taken over by the LNER, it gained the number 5505, the one it carries here when seen near Rugby on 2 February 1929. It was never allocated north of the border but spent most of its thirty-seven years and eight months at Immingham, Northwich, Trafford Park and Sheffield. It was withdrawn from Doncaster on 12 August 1960 with the number 62669.

► GCR 2-8-0 1217, Class 8K

Here we have a locomotive with a bit of history. It was designed by Robinson and built at the North British Locomotive Company in Glasgow in September 1912, entering service in the same month at Annesley shed. In the First World War it was attached to the wartime Railway Operating Division (ROD) for service in Europe. After the war, it resumed service with the GCR, and on 6 March 1926 it became part of the LNER as 6217. It can be seen here at Sheffield Neepsend in 1935.

On Friday, 19 September 1941, it was withdrawn from Annesley shed and fitted with a new boiler. This was before being renumbered War Department 736; it was then shipped with thirty-one 8K-Class members to Egypt and Palestine to join the war effort.

► GCR 2-8-0 1222, Class 8K

We have another ROD locomotive, designed by Robinson, and built at the North British Locomotive Company in Glasgow in October 1912. It was built for the GCR and went into service in that month with the number 1222. During the First World War it was engaged in wartime duties, returning to the GCR in 1918. It then spent five months having a general overhaul at Gorton Works. In 1925 it received the number 6222 when part of the LNER; on 17 November 1946, it received the number 3569. It is seen here on the turntable at King's Cross shortly after. On 30 July 1949, it became part of BR and was numbered 63809. Then, on 22 February 1952, it was reassigned under the War Department's control with the number 040 and shipped to Egypt to replace a Stanier 8F.

◄ GNR 0-6-0 3008, Class J1

Designed by Ivatt and built at Doncaster Works, going into service in October 1908, is a GNR locomotive with the number 8. Its first pre-grouping number was 3008, the number it carried when seen here at Derby shed on 5 May 1946. In September of that year, it became a member of the LNER with the number 5007. On becoming part of BR in October 1949, a six was added, making the number 65007. It was withdrawn from service on 4 February 1952 and scrapped the same month at Doncaster Works.

▲ **GCR 4-6-0 1110, Class B9**

Seen at Manchester London Road in 1921 is Robinson-designed
engine No. 1110. It was one of ten built at Beyer, Peacock & Co.,
going into service in October 1906. It received the LNER number
6110 in April 1924 and BR number 1474 in November 1946.
It was withdrawn from Trafford Park in November 1947 and
scrapped at Gorton Works soon after.

▲ **GCR 2-8-0 1234, Class 8K**

A ROD engine, designed by Robinson and seen with a feedwater heater at Gorton shed in 1922. It was built by the North British Locomotive Company in Glasgow for the GCR and released into service in November 1912 with the number 1234. In October 1927, it received the number 6234 and in December 1946, 3581. On nationalisation, it received the BR number 63581. It was withdrawn from Sheffield Darnall on 10 February 1959 and scrapped at Gorton Works a few days later.

This Robinson-designed locomotive was built at Gorton Works and released into service in August 1904 with the GCR number 2. In August 1925, it was given the LNER No. 5002, and it is seen here with that number at Manchester Central station in 1935. In March 1946, it received the LNER number 7420 and, on nationalisation, 67420. It was Robinson's first suburban and branch-line tank engine. He had already designed similar but smaller 4-4-2Ts for the Waterford, Limerick and Western Railway in Ireland. No. 67420 was withdrawn from Neasden on Saturday, 13 December 1958 and scrapped at Gorton Works two months later.

▶ GNR 4-4-0 1320, Class D2

Here is a locomotive designed by Ivatt and built at Doncaster Works in 1898, going into service in June that year for the GNR with the number 1320. It went through two rebuilds, taking the class numbers to D3 and D2. It was entered into the LNER books and in April 1925 received the number 4320, displaying this when seen here at Stafford station in 1938. In October 1946, the number 2151 was applied and then on nationalisation it became 62151, but this was never carried. In April 1949, it was withdrawn and scrapped with the number 2151 after nearly fifty-one years in service.

▲ GNR 0-6-2T 1745, Class N2

No. 1745 was designed by Gresley and built at the North British Locomotive Company in Glasgow, being fitted with condensing equipment from new. It entered service in February 1921 with the GNR and the number 1745. On becoming part of the LNER in February 1924, it received the number 4745. In January 1947 it became 9524, then with BR a year later, 69524. It was withdrawn on 30 November 1959 from King's Cross and scrapped at Doncaster Works the following month. It is seen here as No. 4745 at King's Cross station on 28 September 1931.

◀ GNR 4-6-2 1470 *Great Northern,*
Class A1

This beautiful and powerful Gresley
locomotive is seen here at Doncaster shed in
1935 after it had received forty-nine days'
general overhaul. The locomotive was built at
Doncaster Works for the GNR in April 1922,
going into service on 4 November 1922, when
it was numbered 1470 and named *Great
Northern.* The numbers changed in LNER
service to 1470N, 4470, 500, 113 and 1470.
On nationalisation, it became 60113.

It was the first locomotive of the fifty-two
A1 locomotives rebuilt from 1 May to
25 September 1945. Thompson designed and
rebuilt it as LNER Thompson-Class A1/1.

It was withdrawn from Doncaster on
19 November 1962 and scrapped there two
months later.

◀ NBR 4-4-0 217, Class 633

A photograph here of Balloch station in 1934
with plenty of period adverts and buildings
that could be seen at small Scottish stations.
A locomotive designed by Matthew Holmes,
locomotive superintendent of the NBR, is
passing through single engine. It was built
at Cowlairs Works, going into service in July
1895. When the NBR became part of the
LNER, the number was changed to 9217. It
was withdrawn in October 1939 from Carlisle
Canal shed and scrapped shortly after.

► **GNR 4-4-2 1413, Class C1; and GNR 4-4-2 259, Class C2**

A pair of GNR engines here double-headed on a passenger train at Peterborough station in August 1929. No. 4413 was designed by Ivatt and built at Doncaster Works, going into service in March 1906 with the number 1413. When in the LNER, it gained the number 1413N on 8 September 1923. This was changed two years later to 4413. It was due to be renumbered 2843 but was withdrawn beforehand on 4 January 1946.

The pilot engine 3259 has the same details as the above except that it started with the number 259 and was built in June 1903. Its LNER number in May 1924 was 3259, and it was withdrawn in October 1943 and scrapped shortly after.

► **GNR 0-6-2T 1751, Class N2**

Here we have a workhorse for the GNR, a member of the N2 Class fitted from new with condensing gear, which was later removed. It is seen here in excellent external condition at Hornsey shed in 1922 with the number 1751, which makes it just a year old. It was designed by Gresley and built at the North British Locomotive Company in Glasgow. On becoming part of the LNER, it held the number 4751, then 9530 in July 1946. On nationalisation, the number was changed to 69530. It was withdrawn from Hornsey at the end of 1959 and scrapped at Stratford Works in January 1960.

◄ GER 4-4-0 1877, Class S46

At Peterborough shed on 24 March 1935 is a very attractive engine designed by James Holden, father of another locomotive designer, Stephen. It was built at Stratford Works, going into service in April 1902 as 1877. At the time of building, the Class S46s were the largest express locomotives working in the GER. In 1924, 1877 became 8877. In February 1928, it was rebuilt as part of the Claud Hamilton-Class D14. The first locomotive in the class was named *Claud Hamilton* after Lord Claud Hamilton, chairman of the GER. The LNER made several changes, including an extended smokebox.

Ian Allan wrote in his history of the GER that, of all the locomotive designs that emerged from Stratford Works in James Holden's reign, the one destined to achieve the greatest fame, beyond question, was the Claud Hamilton type 4-4-0. In June 1946, 8877 was renumbered 2528 and under BR it became 62528. It was withdrawn from Milton Constable on 25 June 1951 and scrapped at Stratford Works soon after.

► NBR 4-4-2 879 *Abbotsford*, Class C10

Standing in Edinburgh Waverley station in 1929 is a powerful locomotive designed by William P. Reid for the NBR and built at the North British Railway Company in Glasgow. It was released into service in August 1906 with the number 879 and named *Abbotsford*. It was rebuilt in September 1920. In April 1925, it became part of the LNER with a class change to C11, and the number was changed to 9879. In November 1936, it was withdrawn from Aberdeen Ferryhill MPD and scrapped shortly after. At this time, metal was required in preparation for the coming war, and almost the whole class of locomotives was scrapped within a year or two.

▲ GNSR 4-4-0 105, Class T

A locomotive that has already been drawn into the LNER with the number 6905, standing at Craigellachie station in April 1946. The engine was designed by J. Johnson and N. Pickersgill for the GNSR and built by Neilson, Reid & Co., going into service in September 1897. In November 1946, the number was changed to 2249. Then, on 22 May 1948, the BR number was tweaked to 62249. It was withdrawn from Keith on 10 October 1950 and scrapped very soon after. It is seen here with the crew posing for the camera.

▲ **GER 4-6-0 1523, Class S69**

Stephen Holden designed this locomotive for the GER; it was built at Stratford Works, going into service in May 1914. In this photograph it is already part of the LNER and is seen at Norwich Thorpe station in May 1931 with the number 8523. It was fitted with the rather ugly ACFI feedwater heaters. They are the large heat-exchanging drums on top of the boiler and look like the backpacks on a hitchhiker, giving the class members the nickname of 'hikers'. The equipment was fitted to many of the class, renamed B12, from December 1927. This one was fitted in December 1927. The principle was that the water would be heated by passing through the exhaust, a French idea that was not aesthetically pleasing to look at and was removed in September 1935. It was an experiment, but the drums did little to save fuel and increased maintenance costs. No. 8523 carried the LNER numbers 7437 and 1523, and at nationalisation it became 61523. It was withdrawn on 21 March 1955 and scrapped at Stratford Works soon after.

▲ **GER 4-6-0 1535, Class S69**

Locomotive 1535 was designed by Stephen Holden and Gresley and built at Stratford Works for the GER. It was built to replace the brand-new 1506, which was written off after an accident at Colchester, Essex, in July 1913. No. 1535 went into service in March 1915. In January 1924, as a member of the LNER, it gained the number 8535. With this identity we see it apparently backing onto a train to act as pilot in Liverpool Street station in 1938. In May 1932 it was one of fifty-five locomotives fitted with the ACFI feedwater heaters as already described; these were removed in October 1935. Over the years, the LNER numbers allocated to the locomotive were 7449 and 1535. On nationalisation, the BR number was 61535, and on withdrawal on 11 November 1959, it could be found at Norwich Thorpe. From there, it went to Stratford Works for scrapping.

Locomotives Built by the London and North Eastern Railway

◀ LNER 4-6-2 2502 *Hyperion*, Class A3

We now look at locomotives built for the LNER, starting with one of Gresley's powerful A3 Class, seen here at Edinburgh Haymarket shed. This one is *Hyperion*, and it was built in July 1934 by Doncaster Works. Its first number in 1934 was 2502; then, on 25 August 1946, it received the number carried here, 37. After nationalisation on 30 October 1948, it became 60037.

It is seen here without the German-type smoke deflectors it would have later in life. *Hyperion* was withdrawn on 12 December 1963 and scrapped at Arnott, Young & Co. in Carmyle in June the following year.

◀ LNER 0-6-0T 1063, Class J50/3

Gresley designed a locomotive for the GNR but it was taken straight into the LNER in December 1926. It was built at Doncaster Works, going into service in the same month. It is seen here at Frodingham shed turntable in 1935, with the crew posing for the photographer. On 21 January 1946, it had its last LNER number, 8963, as nationalisation had arrived, and the number 68963 identified it until withdrawal on 13 February 1962 from Low Moor. It was scrapped at Doncaster Works fifteen days later.

▶ **LNER 4-6-2 2512 *Silver Fox*, Class A4**

Here we have a beautiful train and locomotive on a prestige express, 'The Silver Jubilee'. The train began service in the twenty-fifth year of King George V's reign and comprised two twin sets of articulated coaches, a triplet set, and later a single coach was added, giving the train a total of eight coaches all painted in silver. It was worked between King's Cross and Newcastle and the service started on 30 September 1935, lasting until the start of the Second World War. In this photograph, the train is being hauled by A4-Class *Silver Fox* with the number 2512. It also carried the number 17 and then, finally, 60017. It was retired on 5 December 1963 and was broken up at Doncaster Works. The locomotive appeared in various vibrant colours, as well as the wartime unlined black. It is seen here at King's Cross on 11 May 1938. In August 1936, *Silver Fox*, hauling 'The Silver Jubilee' train, achieved a maximum speed of 113mph. At that time it was the highest speed attained by an ordinary passenger train. George Henry Haygreen was the driver. On each side of the casing is a stainless-steel fox made by Samuel Fox & Co.

▶ **LNER 4-6-2 4498 *Sir Nigel Gresley*, Class A4**

Named after its designer, Sir Nigel Gresley, and displaying the number 7, the locomotive is single engine here at King's Cross on 25 June 1947. It was built at Doncaster Works, going into service on 30 October 1937 with the number 4498. On 12 January 1947, it became No. 7, and on nationalisation the number became 60007. It was withdrawn from Aberdeen Ferryhill on 1 February 1966 and was sold three months later to the A4 Preservation Society. At the time of writing, it belongs to the North Yorkshire Moors Railway (NYMR) and is undergoing an overhaul at the National Railway Museum workshops.

◄ LNER 4-6-2 4496 *Golden Shuttle*, Class A4

Passing through Barnby Moor station in 1936 is Class-A4 *Golden Shuttle*, designed by Gresley for the LNER with the number 4496 and released into service on Saturday, 4 September 1937. It was planned for it to be *Sparrow Hawk*, but that name went to 4463/60018. In 1946 the number was changed to 8, and on nationalisation, it was changed to 60008. At the end of the war in 1945, the name was changed to *Dwight D Eisenhower* in honour of the wartime commander. It was withdrawn on 20 July 1963 from New England, Peterborough. On 27 April 1964, it was shipped to the US for preservation, returning once to the National Railway Museum for the Great Gathering of A4s in 2013. It is now on display in the National Railroad Museum in Green Bay, Wisconsin.

► LNER 4-6-0 8577, Class B12

Built for the GER but released into service in September 1928 into the LNER with the number 8577. Stephen Holden designed it but he died in 1918, aged 47, and further rebuilds involved Gresley and other engineers. In 1942 the number changed to 7491, and then, in 1946, 1577. It entered BR with the number 61577. It is seen here when relatively new with a long goods train near Colchester. After thirty-one years of service, it was withdrawn on 28 September 1959 and scrapped two months later at Stratford Works.

▲ LNER 4-6-2 524 *Herringbone*, Class A2

Gateshead shed on 14 September 1948 is the location for this relatively new and late to the LNER 60524 *Herringbone*. It was designed by the CME of the LNER, Edward Thompson, and built at Doncaster Works, going into service on 26 November 1947 as the Big Four were soon to make way for BR. It was named after a racehorse, as most of the class locomotives were. The original number was 524, becoming 60524 on nationalisation. It was withdrawn from Polmadie on 15 February 1965 and scrapped at Motherwell Machinery and Scrap.

◄ LNER 4-6-2 2578 *Bayardo*, Class A3

Here we have a locomotive designed by Gresley and built at the North British Locomotive Company in Glasgow, at the dawn of the LNER. It went into service on 29 October 1924 with the number 2578 and is seen here near Thirsk in 1937. It was named after a racehorse and was withdrawn from Carlisle Canal on 11 September 1961. Scrapping took place with the BR number 60079 in the same month at Doncaster Works when in for an aborted repair.

◄ LNER 4-6-0 2814 *Castle Hedingham*, Class B17/1

Photographed here at Clacton shed in 1947 with the crew and staff posing for the camera is a locomotive designed by Gresley and Thompson. It was built at Darlington Works, going into service on 23 October 1930. In 1946 it was rebuilt as a B2-Class engine to a design by Thompson. On nationalisation, the number was changed to 61614, and it was withdrawn on 8 June 1969 from Cambridge. Scrapping took place at Stratford Works the same month.

▲ LNER Sentinel Steam Railcar

A different locomotive now in the form of a Sentinel steam railcar. These could be found on minor lines around the country; the CLC had four railcars maintained by the LNER. This one, however, is seen here at New Basford station in 1936. The station was on the Great Central Main Line (GCML) and was closed in 1963. Eighty of these Sentinel units were purchased by the LNER between 1925 and 1932. They were single-car units with the ability to have, as in this case, an additional coach. The last Sentinel was withdrawn in 1948, with none preserved.

▲ LNER 4-6-2-2 10000 'Hush Hush', Class W1

Here we have an experimental locomotive designed by Gresley in collaboration with various other engineering companies, including boilermakers Yarrow & Co. of Glasgow and John Brown Shipyard. It had a high-pressure water-tube boiler, and it was never officially named, but due to the secrecy of its manufacture it was christened the 'Hush Hush'. Its design was based on a Gresley Pacific 4-6-2 chassis, but with an additional axle to take the extra length, making it the only 4-6-2-2 engine to run on British metals. It had a corridor tender, which can now be found on the preserved 4488 *Union of South Africa*. On nationalisation, it was renumbered 60700 and was never named. Two names were considered; one was *British Enterprise*, for which the nameplates were actually cast, and the other was *Pegasus*. It was called the 'Galloping Sausage' by enthusiasts because of the boiler shape. It is seen here in September 1930 at the Wavertree Exhibition. It was withdrawn on 1 June 1959 and scrapped the same month at Doncaster Works.

◄ LNER 2-6-2T 2915, Class V1

This locomotive was built at Doncaster Works for the LNER on 30 June 1931, designed by Gresley. A total of eighty-two V1s were built at Doncaster between 1930 and 1939. No. 2915 had a number change to 7615 in 1946 and then to 67615 with BR. It is seen here passing Edinburgh's Princes Street Gardens in March 1933. It was withdrawn on 29 December 1962 and scrapped eleven months later at Inverurie Works.

► LNER 4-6-2 2003 *Lord President*, Class P2

Standing with its long train of carriages in Newark Northgate station is a powerful P2-Class engine, *Lord President*. It was designed by Gresley and built at Doncaster Works, going into service on 13 June 1936. It was rebuilt in December 1944 under the direction of Thompson. In June 1946, the number was changed to 503, and then 60503 under BR. It was withdrawn on 27 November 1959 from York North and was scrapped at Doncaster Works three days later. It was the first of the class to be withdrawn.

▲ LNER 0-6-0 1289, Class J39

Gresley designed this locomotive for the LNER and it was built at
Darlington Works, going into service on 30 June 1927. It was made
for mixed-traffic work and is seen here at the Lincoln Durham Ox
Crossing in 1937 with a passenger train. Just before nationalisation,
the number was changed to 4739, and then to BR as 64739. It
was withdrawn on Saturday, 3 November 1962 from Annesley and
scrapped in September 1963 at Derby Works.

▲ **LNER 2-6-0 3442** *Maccailein Mor/The Great Marquess*, **Class K4**

Winding its way through the trees at Whistlefield in Argyll and Bute on 23 August 1939 is a locomotive that would one day be quite famous. It was designed by Gresley and built at Darlington Works, going into service on 6 July 1938. It had the number 3442 and the name *The Great Marquiss*, but it was not allowed off Eastfield shed in that guise because the spelling was wrong. So, it was named *Maccailein Mor* when it went to Scotland. The name was changed very quickly to *The Great Marquess*. The number was changed in 1946 to 1994, and then under BR to 61994.

It was built to tackle the West Highland Line with its steep gradients and sharp curves and named after James Graham, 1st Marquess of Montrose. In 1959 five members of the K4 Class were moved to Thornton shed for use on goods trains until 1961, when the withdrawals started. No. 61994 was one of the last to be stood down, on Monday, 18 December 1961. It was purchased directly from BR by Viscount Garnock, and then started a long career with various heritage railways. It is now at the Museum of Scottish Railways at Bo'ness and owned by John Cameron, who also owns the LNER Pacific 60009 *Union of South Africa*.

◄ LNER 2-8-2 2394, Class P1

It is open day here at Canning Town in June 1938, and 2394 sits proudly between an ancient coach and some box vans of indeterminate age. Steps had been set up to enable the public to descend after using the stairs on the other side to enter. The engine was designed by Gresley for the LNER and built at Doncaster Works. The P1 Class comprised just two locomotives, 2393 and 2394, both built in the works. They were two of the most powerful freight locomotives built in Britain, handling 100-wagon coal trains. Because of their size, they were only allowed to work this between New England and Ferme Park. Firemen tried to avoid working them due to the big, voracious firebox. While the engineers were working on plans for a P2, this locomotive had been tested with a semi-fast passenger train from King's Cross to Peterborough. The engine managed 64mph, but the fireman was worn out. In 1942 both were rebuilt and reclassified P1/2. In 1945 the need for such powerful goods engines had eased and they were withdrawn and scrapped at Doncaster. They were the first Gresley locomotives to be removed and scrapped without being ready mechanically. Their boilers went to Gresley A1s 2557 *Blair Athol* and 2565 *Merry Hampton*.

◄ LNER 4-6-2 2579 *Dick Turpin*, Class A3

Named after the famous highwayman, Pacific 2579 stands at Harrogate station in 1936, awaiting the signal to set off. It was designed by Gresley and built at the North British Locomotive Company in Glasgow in November 1924, then released with the name *Dick Turpin* shortly after. The number was changed to 80 on 2 February 1946, and then on nationalisation to 60080. It was withdrawn from Gateshead on 19 November 1964 and scrapped at Drapers of Hull the following month. It has, however, been replicated as a OO gauge model by Hornby.

► **LNER 4-6-0 2805 *Burnham Thorpe*, Class B17**

Torside in the beautiful Peak District is the location of 2805 here in 1939. Like most LNER locomotives, it was designed by the CME Nigel Gresley. It was built at the North British Locomotive Company in Glasgow, going into service on 17 December 1928. The number then was 2805 and the name *Burnham Thorpe*. In April 1938, the name was changed to *Lincolnshire Regiment*. In January 1948, it was rebuilt, becoming BR Class B17/6. Just before nationalisation, the number was changed again to 1605, then to 61605 with BR. It was withdrawn on 15 May 1958 and scrapped the same month at Darlington Works.

► **LNER 4-6-0 2834 *Hinchingbrooke*, Class B17**

Simmering gently here at Gorton Works in 1931 with the driver looking on is Gresley Pacific 2834. It was built at Darlington Works and went into service on 17 June 1931 with the number 2834 and the name *Hinchingbrooke*, after a stately home in Cambridge. In 1946 the number was changed to 1634 and then in 1948 under BR it became 61634. It was rebuilt in 1957 as a BR B17/6, but the following year saw its withdrawal and it was scrapped in August 1958 at Doncaster Works.

▲ LNER 4-6-0 2864 *Liverpool,* Class B17/4

In Manchester Central in April 1946, Gresley Pacific 2864 *Liverpool* is being admired here by an enthusiast and interested passenger. It is awaiting the off for its train, the Manchester to Hull via Sheffield and Doncaster. No. 2864 was built at Robert Stephenson & Hawthorns Ltd and released into service on 15 January 1937 with the name *Liverpool*, after the football team. It was rebuilt in October 1946 to Class B17/6 and withdrawn on 1 June 1960. The same month saw it scrapped at Stratford Works.

▲ LNER 4-4-0 253 *Oxfordshire*, Class D49

A parcels train passing Chaloners Whin near York on 3 August 1936 hauled by Gresley locomotive 253 *Oxfordshire*. It was built at Darlington Works on 30 November 1927 and went into service soon after. Before nationalisation, the number was changed to 2702, then 62702 under BR. It was withdrawn from Leeds Neville Hill on 12 November 1958 and scrapped two months later at Darlington Works.

▲ LNER 0-6-0 2963, Class J39

At Knutsford station in Cheshire is Gresley locomotive 2963. It was built at Darlington Works, going into service on 16 September 1931 at Gorton. Before nationalisation, the number was changed to 4824, then under BR 64824. It was withdrawn from service on 29 March 1960 and scrapped at Gorton Works the following month, although the boiler was retained and used on sister locomotive 64918.

◄ LNER 4-4-0 2757 *Dumfries-shire*, Class D49

The year is 1936 as Gresley locomotive 2757 *Dumfries-shire* stands awaiting the off from Waverley station in Edinburgh. It was completed on 29 March 1929 at Darlington Works, going into service the same year. The pre-nationalisation number was 2732, followed by the BR identity 62732. It was withdrawn on 3 November 1958 from Darlington and scrapped almost immediately at Darlington Works, North Road.

► LNER 4-6-0 1069, Class B1

A quiet day at Darlington shed on 30 July 1947 as Class-B1 1069 stands silently beside a humble pannier tank locomotive. It was designed by Thompson and built at the North British Locomotive Company, Glasgow, going into service at Neville Hill on 26 August 1946. It was given the temporary number E1069 on 26 February 1948 and the BR number 61069 on 29 May 1948. It was withdrawn from York North on 16 August 1963, possibly due to damage in an accident. The following month it was scrapped at Darlington.

▼ LNER 2-6-2 4791, Class V2

At Doncaster shed in 1938 is an almost new Gresley locomotive in sparkling condition. It was built at Darlington Works, going into service at New England, Peterborough, on 23 November 1937. During its LNER days, it carried the numbers 4791, 720 and 820. Then, under BR, it was 60820. It was withdrawn from New England on 20 June 1962 and scrapped at Doncaster Works soon after.

◀ **LNER 2-8-0+0-8-2 2395, Class U1**

Here we have a heavy goods engine and the only one in its class; it was designed for banking coal trains at Worsborough Bank, also known as the Worsborough Incline, which climbs for 7 miles. The locomotive was planned during GCR days and was based on two GCR 8K 2-8-0s. No attempt had been made to build such a locomotive. In 1923, when the GCR became part of the LNER with Nigel Gresley as CME, it was looked at again. Beyer, Peacock & Co. in Manchester quoted £21,000 for two such locomotives, but the order was reduced to just one. It cost £14,895 and was delivered in 1925. Still in primer paint, it was taken to the centenary exhibition of the S&DR with exhibit number 42. The locomotive was given the number 2395 and assisted the heavy goods trains on the Worsborough Bank on around eighteen return trips a day. The staff did not appreciate the extra effort needed to operate such a large engine. There were two tunnels at the top of the bank, and 2395 would be the third engine to enter the smoke-filled tunnels, making the atmosphere on the footplate almost unbearable; it was described as being 'close to hell'. As a result, gas masks were issued to the crew!

It was numbered 9999 by the LNER and then 69999 by BR. After some work, it returned to banking the Worsborough Bank, but in 1952 it went into storage at Gorton Works. Experiments with a conversion to oil burning were tried while there, and it returned to work the Lickey Incline. By 23 December of that year, it was withdrawn and taken to Doncaster Works to be cut up. It had been in service for thirty years and travelled 425,000 miles. It is seen here by the turntable at Mexborough shed in July 1935.

◀ **LNER 0-4-0T 87, Class Y3**

Seen here at March shed in 1938 is a Sentinel steam shunter. These useful marshalling yard tools came in classes Y1 and Y3. The Y1 Class had one speed, the Y3, which this is, had two speeds. A total of thirty-two Y3s were purchased between 1927 and 1931, and all had a large boiler. The big companies trialled the Y3 steam shunter, but the LNER made the most use of them. They were based on the Sentinel steam wagons that were in use until the 1950s. All Y3 shunters for the LNER were built at the Sentinel Wagon Works and introduced in 1927. No. 87 was withdrawn and scrapped in 1955.

▲ **LNER 0-6-0 1286, Class J39**

St Mary le Wigford, the eleventh-century church in Lincoln, is seen here in 1937, where Class-J39 1286 passes by with a train of somewhat antiquated carriages. It was built at Doncaster Works, going into service at Copley Hill, Leeds, on 23 June 1927 for the LNER. In 1946 the number was changed to 4737, and then with BR 64737. It was withdrawn from Doncaster on 15 August 1959 and scrapped there the following month.

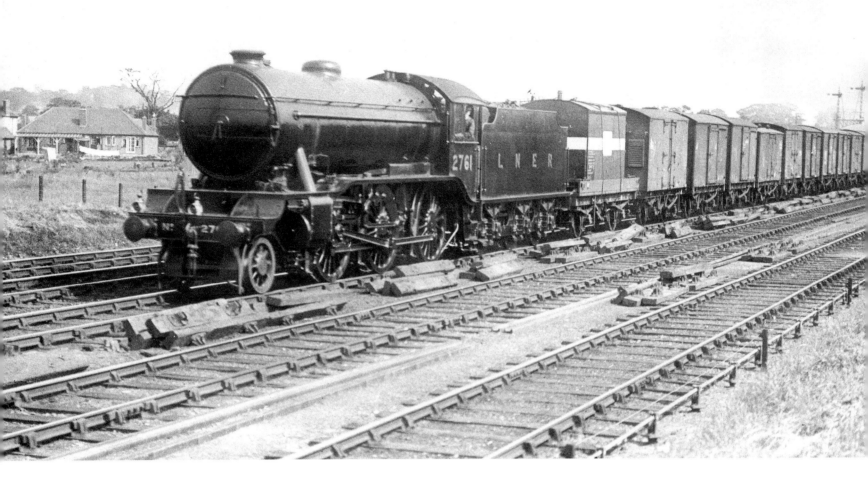

▲ **LNER 2-6-0 2761, Class K3**

Photographed near Potters Bar with a train of box vans is an engine designed by Gresley for the LNER. It was built at Darlington Works and released into service in July 1930 with the number 2761. In September 1946, it was allocated No. 1890, and, during nationalisation, was given the BR number 61890. It was withdrawn on 16 September 1962 after a service life of thirty-two years, two months and seventeen days. It was scrapped in July 1963 at Cashmore's of Great Bridge.

◄ **LNER 2-6-0 4830, Class V2**

This locomotive was designed by Gresley and built at Darlington Works for the LNER. It was released into service on 18 May 1939 to Leicester with the number 4830. It is seen here at Staverton Road in North Oxfordshire in 1946. On 7 November 1946, it was allocated No. 859 and it received the BR number 60859 during nationalisation. It was withdrawn on 20 September 1965 from Gateshead. It was scrapped in October 1965 at Ellis Metals in Swalwell, Gateshead.

THE SOUTHERN RAILWAY (SR)

Locomotives in companies drawn into the Southern Railway on amalgamation:

London, Brighton and South Coast Railway (LBSCR): 457 miles (736km)
London and South Western Railway (LSWR): 1,020 miles (1,642km)
South Eastern and Chatham Railway Managing Committee (SECR) (an amalgamation of South Eastern Railway, and London, Chatham and Dover Railway): a total of 637 miles (1,026km)

There were six low-mileage subsidiary companies amalgamated with the above:

Croydon and Oxted Joint Railway
Dover and Deal Railway
Epsom and Leatherhead Railway (ELR)
Portsmouth and Ryde Railway
Tooting, Merton and Wimbledon Railway (TM&WR)
Woodside and South Croydon Joint Railway (W&SC)

Locomotives in Companies Drawn into the Southern Railway on Amalgamation

◀ LBSCR 4-4-2 423 *The Needles*, Class H2

London Bridge station in 1947, and standing at the platform having just brought in a train is one of Douglas Marsh's powerful Atlantics. It was built at Brighton Works, going into service in September 1911 with the number 423. On becoming part of the SR, it received the number as shown here, 2423. It did receive the BR number 32423 but never carried it as it was the first and only member of the class to be withdrawn before entering BR. It was scrapped on 30 June 1949.

◄ **LBSCR 0-6-0T 40** *Brighton*, **Class A1**

Designed by William Stroudley, this locomotive was one of his 'Stroudley Terriers' built for the LBSCR in 1878. It was initially given the number 40 and was chosen to represent the LBSCR in that year's Paris Exhibition. It was taken to Paris and made many runs around France, demonstrating its Westinghouse air brake system. It won a gold medal for its design, workmanship and finish.

It was returned to England and was allocated to Battersea shed with a spell working on the sea defences at Newhaven. In 1902, after being deemed surplus to requirements, it was overhauled at Brighton Works, given the number 11 and sold to the Isle of Wight Central Railway (IWCR). Isle of Wight Railway No. 11 is seen here at Newport station on 29 March 1930. No. 11.

It arrived there on 8 January 1902. On amalgamation in 1923, the IWCR became part of the SR and No. 11 was given the number W11 and, in 1930, the name *Newport*. In April 1946, it was taken out of service and stored until February 1947, when it was taken back to England for overhaul at Eastleigh. While there, nationalisation arrived, and it joined BR with the number 32640.

It started working along the south coast, in particular, the Hayling Island branch. In 1963 it was withdrawn, then purchased by Billy Butlin and placed as a static exhibit at his Pwllheli holiday camp. It remained there until 1973, when it was purchased by Sir Peter Allen, president of the Wight Locomotive Society; the society had hoped that they would acquire a Terrier for the island. In 1973 it was conveyed to the island and started a refurbishment period from being a static exhibit to a beautifully turned-out locomotive. It went through various paint schemes, one displaying the BR logo and its old number 32640. In 2020 it was taken in for service and is now back vibrantly painted and a credit to the organisation.

◄ **LSWR 0-4-2 644, Class A12**

A locomotive designed by William Adams and built at Neilson, Reid & Co. in Glasgow is seen here, passing Gosport shed. It was built in March 1893 and, on amalgamation, retained its number within the SR. It was withdrawn in January 1939, but it was retained as a stationary boiler at Eastleigh Works in October. Final withdrawal and scrapping came in August 1945 at Eastleigh Works.

▶ **LSWR 4-6-0 462, Class T14**

Sitting alongside the coaling plant at Nine Elms shed in London on 20 May 1932 is a Dugald Drummond-designed locomotive. It was built at Eastleigh Works, going into service with the LSWR in 1912. It was one of only ten locomotives in the class, and six of them joined BR, but only for a short time; all had gone by 1951. The LSWR number was retained throughout its time in the SR, and the BR number 30462 was issued but never carried. However, it was rebuilt in August 1930, and it was one of the last of the class withdrawn in February 1950 and scrapped at Eastleigh Works. The enthusiasts' nicknames for it were 'Paddleboxes' or 'Paddleboats'.

◀ **LBSCR 4-4-0 45, Class B4X**

No. 45 was designed by L. Billinton for the LBSCR and built at Brighton Works, being released for service in June 1902. In 1911 the Drummond water-tube firebox with which it had initially been fitted was removed. It was rebuilt in April 1923 as a B4X-Class locomotive, and it carried the number 45 into the SR, later having it changed to 2045. It is seen here at New Cross shed in 1932.

No. 2045 was the last representative of the B4X Class and was withdrawn from Bricklayers Arms on 12 May 1951. On nationalisation, the locomotive was allocated the BR number 32045 but never carried it. It was scrapped the following year.

◄ **LBSCR 4-6-0 333** *Remembrance,* **Class L**

A locomotive built by the LBSCR in April 1922. It was built as the LBSCR War Memorial Locomotive commemorating the 532 men of the company who died in the Great War. As well as the name *Remembrance*, a plaque was affixed below the name displaying a tribute to the 532 men who died. The locomotive, with SR number 2333, is seen here leaving Victoria station on 31 December 1932 with the Southern Belle. It was built at Brighton Works to a design by Maunsell and released into service in April 1922; in June 1935, it was rebuilt. In April 1948, it received the BR number 32333 and was withdrawn from Basingstoke on 30 April 1956 and scrapped at Brighton Works in the same month.

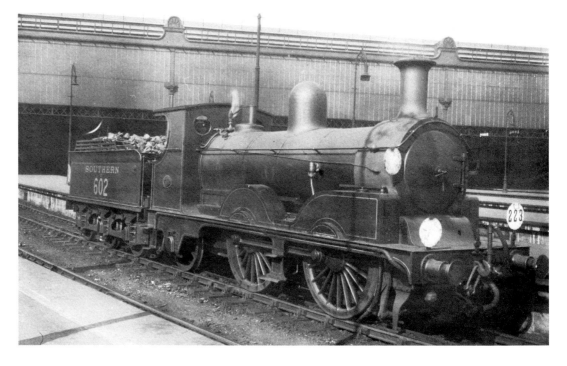

► **LSWR 0-4-2 602, Class A12**

Designed by Adams, one of a class of ninety locomotives built for the LSWR, No. 602 was built at Nine Elms Works in March 1894. It retained its number through the SR years, was withdrawn in July 1933 and scrapped at Eastleigh Works shortly after; none of the class locomotives were preserved. It is seen here at Waterloo station on 29 June 1932.

▲ LSWR 0-4-0T 229 and 177, Class O2

Two locomotives of the O2 Class stand at Melcombe Regis station on the Portland Branch Railway. Adams designed both, and they were built at Nine Elms Works, No. 229 in December 1892 and No. 177 in December 1889. The numbers remained the same while in the SR, and under BR, 229 became 30229 and 177, 30177. No. 30229 was withdrawn on 31 March 1961 and 30177 on 3 October 1959. Both were scrapped soon after withdrawal at Eastleigh Works.

▲ **SECR 0-6-0 654, Class B2**

A William Kirtley-designed locomotive built at the Vulcan Foundry in November 1891 stands at Gillingham shed in July 1931.

It retained its pre-grouping number through its time in the SR but never reached BR, being withdrawn in March 1933 from Gillingham, and scrapped at Ashford Works in the December of that year.

Robertsbridge station yard on 22 July 1935
is the background to this Harry Wainwright-
designed locomotive. It was built at Ashford
Works in March 1901 and retained the
number 1037 throughout its time in the SR.
Going into BR with the number 31037, it was
withdrawn on 25 February 1961 and scrapped
the following month at Ashford Works.

► SECR 0-4-4T 1519, Class H

Here we have another Harry Wainwright
engine built at Ashford Works in July 1909
and going into service the same month.
No. 1519 is seen here passing the Swanley
signal box entering the station. On amalgamation, the number was changed to 31519. It
was withdrawn in February 1961 and scrapped
at Ashford Works three months later.

▲ SECR 2-6-0 1815, Class N

A shot of Reigate station and the busy road crossing in 1938, as Maunsell-designed locomotive No. 1815 lets off steam before pulling away. The locomotive was built at Ashford Works in December 1920 and went into service with the number 1815. Three years later, it became part of the SR with the same number. On nationalisation, it was renumbered 31815 and was withdrawn on 26 May 1963, then scrapped two months later.

► **LSWR 4-4-0 337, Class T9**

One of Dugald Drummond's engines. They were nicknamed 'greyhounds' due to their excellent turn of speed. The crews were also happy with them. This example was built at Nine Elms for the LSWR, going into service in October 1901. It maintained that number through amalgamation and until nationalisation, when the number carried was 30337. The long service life of fifty-seven years came to an end when it was withdrawn in November 1958 and scrapped at Eastleigh Works. It is seen here on 8 June 1933 at Worplesdon, Surrey.

◄ **LBSCR 0-6-0T 84 *Crowborough*, Class A1**

LBSCR locomotive No. 84 *Crowborough*, built in 1880 at Brighton, was sold to the IWCR in November 1903 for £725 and given the number 12 and the name *Ventnor*. It was rebuilt to A1X standard in July 1916 and fitted for push-and-pull working in February 1926. On grouping, it became part of the SR, working on the Isle of Wight. It was withdrawn in October 1935 and scrapped at Eastleigh in March 1949. It is seen here at Newport shed on the Isle of Wight in 1932.

◄ LSWR 4-6-0 444, Class T14

Another look at a Dugald Drummond T14, built at Eastleigh Works in May 1911 for the LSWR. It retained its number throughout its time with the SR. It was one of only ten in the class, built for express passenger duties on the LSWR. It was rebuilt in 1931 and is seen here at Worplesdon on 8 June 1933. On nationalisation, it was with BR for a year, being given the number 30444. However, this was never applied as it was withdrawn from Nine Elms on 28 February 1950 and scrapped at Eastleigh Works.

► LBSCR 2-6-0 344, Class K

We have a powerful mixed-traffic locomotive blowing off steam at Brighton station on 20 August 1932. Designed by Robert Billinton for the LBSCR with the number 344, it was built at Brighton Works and entered service in December 1916. When a member of the SR, the number was 2344, and on nationalisation, it went into BR with the number 32344. After forty-six years of hard work, it was withdrawn from Brighton and scrapped at Eastleigh Works on 31 January 1963.

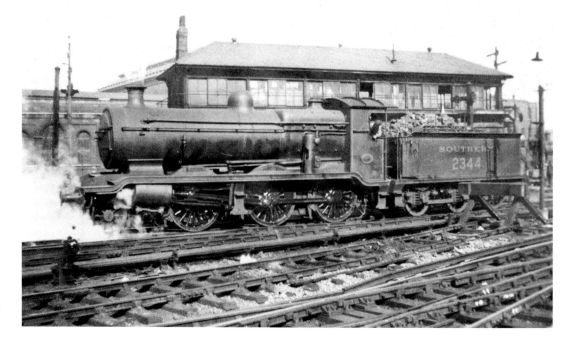

▶ LSWR 4-4-0 299, Class C8

Here, on Monday, 3 March 1930, C8 No. 299, with 8-wheel water-cart tender, is awaiting departure for Salisbury at London Waterloo station. It was originally built for the Bournemouth express service, but it was not capable of keeping to timetable and was consequently relegated to less important trains. It was built in the LSWR works at Nine Elms and entered service in November 1898. It was shedded at Nine Elms before being transferred in 1932 to Fareham for Sunday excursion traffic. It never had a number change except for the addition of a small 'E' above the number upon joining the SR, but this was removed by 1932. It was withdrawn and cut up at Eastleigh Works in August 1938.

▼ LBSCR 0-6-0T 61 *Sutton*, Class A1

At Havant station is one of the popular 'Stroudley Terriers', named because of the noise they made. The Hayling Island branch, with its weak bridge, is where they could be seen, as well as on the Isle of Wight. This one was built in October 1875 at Brighton Works with the LBSCR number and name 61 *Sutton*, then B661, followed by the number shown here, 2661. It was rebuilt in January 1912 with the class number A1X. In May 1951, it became part of BR with the number 32661.

The Terriers were popular on the commuter routes around London, but these handy light engines, when no longer required, were sold off to various private enterprises. Still, with their many small branch lines, some of the Terriers sold were repurchased when the SR took over. The class was designed by William Stroudley and comprised sixty members built between 1874 and 1880 at Brighton Works. This one, however, was rebuilt when Douglas Earl Marsh was the carriage and wagon superintendent of the LBSCR. It entered BR with the number 32661 and continued to give good service until withdrawn on 28 October 1963. In November that year the bridge over Langstone Harbour to Hayling Island closed. This little locomotive was scrapped at Eastleigh Works six months later.

▲ **LSWR 2-4-0WT 298, Class 298**

Under the winch at Wadebridge shed in July 1931 is a Beattie-designed well tank locomotive that bears the number of the class when first built, 298. It was initially built by Beyer, Peacock & Co. in June 1874 and released into service shortly after.

The number changed to 0298 under the SR, and on nationalisation it was renumbered 30587 as part of BR. Adams rebuilt it from 1884 to 1892, Urie from 1921 to 1922 and Maunsell from 1931 to 1935. It was one of several similar locomotives retained for use on the Wenford Bridge china clay trains. On 31 December 1962, it was withdrawn from Wadebridge shed after a remarkably long life of eighty-eight and a half years, but it did not end there; it was preserved by the Bodmin and Wenford Railway, where it now lives and works, painted beautifully in unlined black. The boiler ticket expires in 2023, so it has certainly been rewarded for its long life of hard work on the metals.

▲ **LSWR 0-4-4T 211, Class O2**

Ryde Esplanade in 1932 sees an ex-LSWR engine, W20 *Shanklin*. This Adams-designed locomotive was built at Nine Elms Works in March 1892 for the LSWR with the number 211. In February 1925, it received the SR number W20. In 1924 it was transferred to the Isle of Wight and continued to work there until withdrawal in 1966. This was after seventy-four years and six months in service. It was scrapped shortly after withdrawal.

◄ LBSCR 4-4-0 47 *Canada*, Class B4

A smart Robert Billinton-designed locomotive is seen here looking clean and polished at Brighton shed in 1922. The class was built to haul heavy express trains on the LBSCR but was relegated in 1912 when more powerful engines started working. Rail writer O.S. Knock was heard to describe the class as 'being amongst the finest locomotives of their day'. This member of the class was built at Sharp, Stewart & Co. for the LBSCR and went into service with the name and number 47 *Canada*. The SR renumbered it B47 and 2047, withdrawal came on 31 July 1937 and it was scrapped at Eastleigh Works on 30 April 1938.

► LBSCR 4-4-0 B315, Class B2X

Simmering quietly at Horsted Keynes station on 8 January 1932 is engine number B315. The first carriage on the train is the birdcage variety, designed by Robert Billinton and built at Brighton Works on 30 June 1895. Their nickname was 'grasshopper'. B315 was rebuilt from Class B2 in March 1909. Robert Billinton had become the CME in 1890 after the sudden death of his predecessor, William Stroudley. In the SR, 315 became 2315, and as a result of the line being electrified, it was withdrawn on 30 April 1933. Scrapping followed at Brighton Works shortly after.

▲ SECR 0-6-0T A557, Class P

A perfect period photograph of a goods train passing families sitting with just a low railing between them and the line. The location was Dover in June 1932. The engine, looking rather shabby, was built at Ashford Works in February 1909. It was designed by Harry Wainwright and was loosely based on the Stroudley Terrier.

On amalgamation, it received the number SR 1557, but not until 1933. This number was retained with a three added, making it 31557 when part of BR. It was withdrawn from Stewarts Lane on Saturday, 21 September 1957. Then, after forty-eight years and seven months of service, it was scrapped at Ashford Works.

▲ **LBSCR 4-4-2T 89, Class 13**

Douglas Earl Marsh and Robert Billinton designed this locomotive class
for the LBSCR. It went into service in December 1912 with the number
89 and it became SR 2089 on amalgamation. It is seen here with a
short local train at The Dyke station. This station is now long gone but
was then on the line from The Dyke Junction station (now Aldrington
station). At the time the photo was taken, it was a significant tourist
destination at the foot of Devil's Dyke. When the line was opened, it
was the Brighton and Dyke Railway. The locomotive entered BR with
the number 32089 and was withdrawn from Eastbourne on 30 April
1951. The following day it arrived at Eastleigh Works for scrapping.

▲ **LSWR 0-4-4T 328, Class M7**

Here we have a spick-and-span member of the M7 Class, No. 328, sitting at the exit to Exmouth shed. It was designed by Dugald Drummond and built at Eastleigh Works, going into service in November 1911. Under BR, the number was changed to 30328 in 1950. It was withdrawn from Tunbridge Wells on 31 March 1963 and scrapped at Eastleigh Works three months later.

◄ **SECR 0-4-4T 1308, Class H**

An interesting view of locomotive No. 1308 passing through Sharnal Street station. This station, situated on the Hundred of Hoo branch in Kent, was closed in 1961. Hopefully, a new station will be built nearby to take high-speed trains. As for the locomotive, it was designed by Harry Wainwright and built at Ashford Works for the SECR. It went into service in June 1906, retaining its number through to nationalisation. Under BR, the number was changed to 31308, and it was withdrawn in December 1962 and scrapped a year later.

◄ **SECR 4-4-0 315, Class F1**

Standing in the yard at Bricklayers Arms shed on 18 May 1929 is a locomotive designed by Dugald Drummond and built at Dubs & Co. On going into service in May 1897, the number was 315, and this was retained through induction into the SR. On nationalisation, the number became BR 30315; then, on 31 December 1962, it was withdrawn from Salisbury. Seven months later, it was scrapped at Eastleigh Works.

▲ **LSWR 4-4-2T 520, Class Radial Tanks**

Lyme Regis station in 1938 sees 4-4-2T 3520 passing through with a small train. Designed by Adams and built by Dubs & Co., the locomotive went into service in December 1885 with the number 520. On amalgamation in 1922, the number was changed to 0520; then, the SR changed to numbers E0520 and 30520. On coming under the banner of BR, it acquired the identity 30584. Most of the class locomotives were withdrawn after the First World War, but three members of this obsolete class were retained to work the Lyme Regis Branch. One of them was this one, which carried the number 3520. It was eventually withdrawn on Saturday, 28 January 1961 after seventy-five years of service. It was scrapped at Eastleigh Works in December that year.

▲ **LBSCR 4-4-0 54 *Empress*, Class B4A**

Stopped at Oxted station in 1931 is Class-B4A locomotive
2054, designed by Robert Billinton for the LBSCR and going
into service with the number 54 in May 1900 with the name
Empress. Then, in 1906, the name was changed to *Princess
Royal*. It was built at Brighton Works. On amalgamation with
the SR, it first carried the number B54, then the one shown
here, 2054. The BR number 32054 was never carried as it was
withdrawn in June 1951 and scrapped very soon after.

Locomotives Built by the Southern Railway

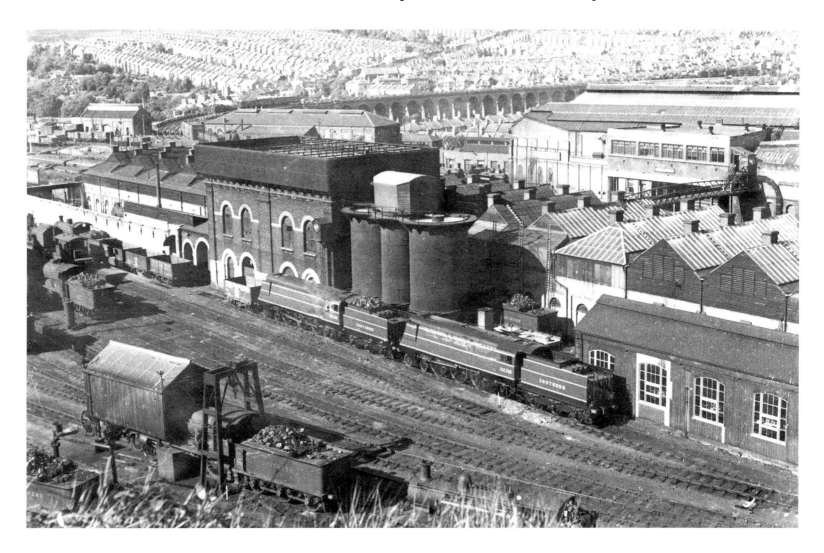

▲ SR 4-6-2 21C135 *Shaftesbury* and 4-6-2 21C136 *Westward Ho*, Class West Country/Battle of Britain

Here we start our look at the locomotives built for the SR with a two-for-one offer. We have a panoramic view across Brighton shed to the London Road railway viaduct. This viaduct was built in 1846, comprised twenty-seven arches and was designed by John Urpeth Rastrick.

But back to the locomotives standing silently at the Brighton shed displaying their SR logo and streamlined, air-smoothed casing. They were both designed

by Bulleid and built at Brighton Works in July 1946. *Shaftesbury* received the BR number 34035 on nationalisation in 1949. It was withdrawn on 8 June 1963 and scrapped in April 1964 at Eastleigh Works.

Westward Ho received the number 34036 on nationalisation, and in 1960 it was rebuilt, at which time the streamlining was removed. It was withdrawn on 9 July 1967 and scrapped at Cashmore's of Newport.

◄ SR 0-8-0T 955, Class Z

At Ashford shed on 30 June 1934 is a powerful tank engine built for heavy shunting and local work. It was designed by Maunsell and built at Brighton Works, going into service in July 1929. On nationalisation, the number became 30955; it was withdrawn from Exmouth Junction in December 1962 and scrapped on 20 January 1963 at Eastleigh Works.

► SR Electric 2014, Class 4Lav

This class of electric railcars was built at Eastleigh Works in October 1936. The railcars were for use on the London to Brighton line that had just been electrified. The Class 4Lav indicates the number of lavatories, although this is a bit of a misnomer as the four-car set had only one. The set was made up of a power car, two trailer cars and then another power car. No. 2014 is seen here at Hastings in July 1935, but it enjoyed a short life as it was destroyed at Brighton at 12.21 p.m. on 25 May 1943 by enemy action in the Second World War. The Depot and Pullman shops were bombed, as was a span of the London Road viaduct.

▲ SR 4-6-0 855 *Robert Blake*, Class Lord Nelson

We have here a Lord Nelson-Class locomotive stopped at Dover
Harbour station in June 1931, awaiting the off. It was designed
by Maunsell and built at Eastleigh Works in December 1928.
On nationalisation, the number was changed to 30855; it was
withdrawn on 30 September 1961 and scrapped in February the
following year. It was later built as a OO scale model by Bachmann.

▲ SR 4-4-0 932 *Blundells*, Class V Schools

Southampton Central in 1939 and a Bournemouth to Waterloo train stands at
the platform. Designed by Maunsell and built at Eastleigh Works, 932 *Blundells*
went into service in February 1935. It was fitted with a self-trimming, high-sided
tender from 1938 to 1958. Under BR, it became 30932, and it was withdrawn
in February 1961 for scrapping at Ashford Works in July 1961. This is another
engine replicated as a OO model by Hornby.

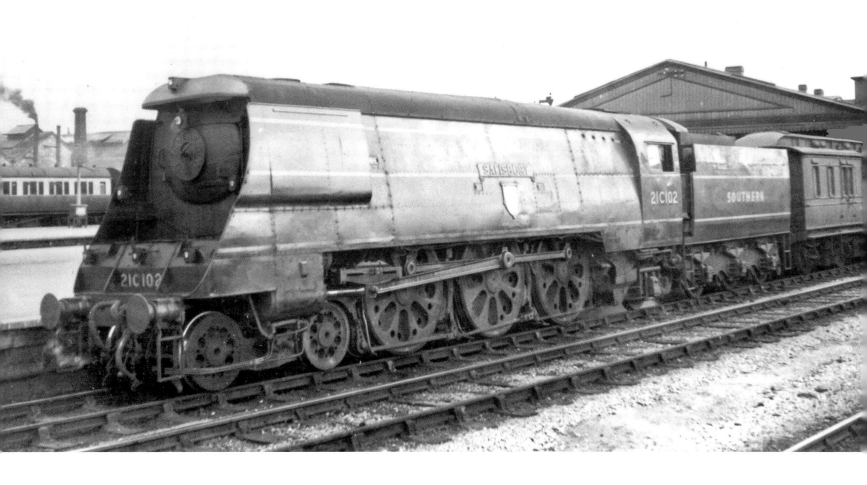

▲ SR 4-6-2 21C102 *Salisbury*, Class West Country/Battle of Britain

Newton Abbot station in 1947 is the location of Bulleid-designed light Pacific West Country/Battle of Britain-Class locomotive, 21C102. The locomotive was built at Brighton Works in June 1945 and named *Salisbury* on 11 July 1946. On nationalisation, it became 34002. *Salisbury* has been preserved and is now the oldest surviving Bulleid Pacific in original condition. It was allocated to Exmouth Junction from 1948 to 1964. In January 1965, 34002 was moved to Nine Elms, where it worked the last steam express service on BR. It was withdrawn in April 1967 and was being transferred to Newport for scrapping.

Fortunately, this did not happen as George Salisbury intervened and had it taken to Salisbury shed, where he paid BR £2,750 for it. It remained at Salisbury until the shed was demolished in 1969, at which time it was taken to Eastleigh for overhaul. It was the last steam engine to be overhauled by BR. It returned to steam in 1971 and spent seven years running main-line specials. It failed after this and spent time as a static display exhibit. Repairs were carried out, and it was returned to hauling trains on the Bathcombe Railway and to making guest appearances on other preserved lines. It now comes under the Mainline Bulleid Trust and is back on the metals.

◄ SR 0-6-0 C31, Class Q1

The war is over, yet this locomotive built not for its good looks but to help with the war effort stands at Battersea station in 1947. Before the war, the SR was mainly a high-density passenger railway and had no goods engines, unlike the other three companies. In 1939 plans were set to build a heavier engine capable of serving the area closest to Europe as cheaply as possible and capable of heavy goods work. Initially, the Q1 Class was developed by Maunsell and then, after his retirement in 1938, Bulleid.

The Q1 Class consisted of just forty locomotives and had many labour-saving devices to suit the wartime austerity. The class acquired many nicknames such as 'Ugly Ducklings', 'Coffee Pots', 'Charlies', 'Biscuit Tins' and 'Frankensteins'. Although rough and ready, the class locomotives served the SR well and were able to punch above their weight to haul heavy wartime goods and passenger trains. This carried on post-war, and the last one was withdrawn in 1966. The first member was numbered Q1 and is now in the Railway Museum at York. Bulleid designed C31, and it was built at Ashford Works, going into service in October 1942. In July 1949, it was given the BR number 33031. It was withdrawn on Sunday, 29 September 1963 and scrapped in July 1964.

◄ SR 4-4-0 905 *Tonbridge*, Class V Schools

The suitably named 905 *Tonbridge* can be seen here in 1938 at Tonbridge shed. On nationalisation, it would acquire the BR number 30905 in October 1949. Maunsell designed the locomotive, and it was built at Eastleigh Works, going into service in May 1930. It was withdrawn on Saturday, 9 December 1961 and scrapped at Eastleigh Works. One of the nameplates is exhibited in the physics department of Tonbridge School. Most of the schools mentioned in the class were given a nameplate on withdrawal.

▲ SR 4-4-0 925 *Cheltenham*, Class V Schools

Standing at the platform at Southampton Central with the Bournemouth to Newcastle train is V Schools-Class locomotive No. 925. It was designed by Maunsell and built at Eastleigh Works, being released into service in April 1934. In May 1950, it was numbered BR 30925. *Cheltenham* was withdrawn in December 1962 and chosen for preservation by the National Collection. There followed a period of overhaul and work on the main line as soon as it became legal. It is now on location with the Mid-Hants Railway and was due for an overhaul when the operational boiler ticket ran out in 2022. Now in vibrant SR Malachite Green, it is one of a well-regarded class of locomotives.

▲ SR 4-6-2 21C157 *Biggin Hill*, **Class West Country/Battle of Britain**

The Golden Arrow express leaves Dover Harbour in 1947 while two trainspotters get dazzled by the sun. The hard-working locomotive is 21C157 *Biggin Hill*. The Bulleid-designed engine was built at Brighton Works and released into service in March 1947. On 25 June 1949, it received the BR number 34057, which it retained until withdrawal on Sunday, 7 May 1967. It was scrapped in October 1967 by Cashmore's of Newport. The locomotive was named after RAF Biggin Hill, a vital RAF station during the Second World War and now a civil airport with a small air force presence.

◄ SR 4-6-2 21C127 *Taw Valley*, Class West Country/Battle of Britain

Seen in 1948 is ex-SR locomotive 34027 *Taw Valley* standing light engine at Exeter Central. The Bulleid-designed locomotive was built at Brighton Works, going into service in March 1946 with the number 21C127. On 1 August 1948, it was photographed here just after it was taken into BR as 34027. On 13 September 1957, it was rebuilt at Eastleigh Works, at which time the air-smoothed streamlining was removed along with other modifications. On Sunday, 9 August 1964, it was withdrawn from Salisbury.

Shortly after, it was towed to Woodhams scrapyard at Barry, where it languished with many others awaiting either rescue or scrapping. Fortunately, it was rescued in 1980 by Barry Hitchen in a sad state after nearly twenty years in the open. It was taken to the NYMR, where restoration began. Later, it was moved to the East Lancashire Railway (ELR), then in 1985 to the Severn Valley Railway (SVR), where restoration continued. It went into service on the SVR in 1988, carrying out main-line duties, including hauling the Orient Express on day running around the Southern Region from London and other destinations such as Portsmouth. Other express workings were the Cumbrian Mountain Express, the North Wales Coast Express and the Welsh Marches Express. Then, of course, the Hogwarts Express. In 2005 it was withdrawn for a complete overhaul. At the time of writing, it is working on the SVR lines but not on the main line.

◄ SR 4-6-2 21C9 *Shaw Savill*, Class Merchant Navy

Awaiting to depart Exeter Central station in 1946 is a member of the Bulleid Pacific Merchant Navy Class. 21C9 *Shaw Savill* was built at Eastleigh Works in June 1942. It is seen here recently painted in Southern Malachite green livery, a change from its original wartime black. There is some slight crash damage to the tender done before the repaint. To see complete and comprehensive details of this now preserved locomotive, turn to page 124.

▲ SR 4-6-0 865 *Sir John Hawkins*, **Class Lord Nelson**

Woking station in July 1939, and we see Lord Nelson-Class locomotive 865, *Sir John Hawkins*. It was designed by Maunsell and built at Eastleigh Works, to be released into service in November 1929. Under BR, the number was changed to 30865, and it was withdrawn from service on Saturday, 20 May 1961. It was the last of the class scrapped but one was preserved, 850 *Lord Nelson*.

► SR 4-6-0 857 *Lord Howe,*
Class Lord Nelson

At Waterloo station and the end of the
platform, 857 *Lord Howe* awaits the off on
18 June 1932. Designed by Maunsell and
built at Eastleigh Works, it entered service
in December 1928. It was withdrawn on
26 September 1962 and scrapped the
following month.

◄ SR 4-4-0 904 *Lancing,* Class V Schools

Lancing, in the countryside near Battle, is the
location of No. 904 *Lancing* on 25 July 1935.
It is another Maunsell locomotive, built at
Eastleigh Works and going into service in
May 1930. Under BR, the number became
30904 in July 1948. It was withdrawn from
Basingstoke on 31 July 1961 and scrapped at
Ashford Works two months later.

▲ **SR 2-6-0 1894, Class U1**

Typical enamel advertising forms a backdrop at Exeter St Davids station in 1938 as Mogul No. 1894 passes with a goods train. The engine was designed by Maunsell and built at Eastleigh Works in 1931 for the SR. The class was U1, receiving the nickname 'U-boats' after the German submarines. It was withdrawn on 30 December 1962 and scrapped in May the following year.

► SR Electric 2007, Class 4LAV

A pretty common sight on SR tracks as electric traction took over, No. 2007 is seen at Hastings in July 1935. It went into service on 16 March 1935 and was withdrawn to Lancing for repair after an accident on 2 March 1944 with class member 2928. It went back into service on 4 July 1944. On 2 July 1961 it was taken back in for repairs to the cab and offside front damage after an accident and it was fixed at Lancing four months later. On 8 June 1968, it was damaged by fire at Brighton. On 22 November 1969 it went to the Bird Group at Long Marston for scrapping.

◄ SR 4-6-2 21C14 *Nederland Line*, Class Merchant Navy

Bulleid Merchant Navy-Class *Nederland Line* stands at Waterloo station in 1947 with the Devon Belle express. The locomotive was built at Eastleigh Works and went into service in February 1945. In May 1949, it entered BR with the number 35014, and at the same time, the cab was replaced. In September 1956, it was rebuilt, during which time the air-smoothed casing was removed. It was withdrawn on Sunday, 26 March 1967 and scrapped at Cashmore's of Newport.

▲ SR 4-6-0 853 *Sir Richard Grenville*, Class Lord Nelson

No. 853 is at Weald on the Victoria Dover Boat Train, the job that
the class was built for. It was travelling via the Orpington loop. Lord
Nelson No. 853 was designed by Maunsell and built at Eastleigh
Works, going into service in September 1928. On becoming part
of BR, it received the number 30853. The class consisted of sixteen
members, all named after Royal Navy admirals. No. 30853 was
withdrawn on Saturday, 3 March 1962 and scrapped the following
month. Only class leader *Lord Nelson* was preserved.

▲ SR 4-6-0 855 *Robert Blake*, **Class Lord Nelson**

The spectacular frontage of Dover Harbour station in June 1931 as a Maunsell locomotive pulls away with a passenger train. The engine was built at Eastleigh Works, going into service in November 1928. On coming under BR, it received the number 30855. *Robert Blake* was withdrawn on Saturday, 30 September 1961 and scrapped in February 1962. It is now a OO scale model made by Bachmann.

◀ SR 4-4-0 926 *Repton*, Class V Schools

V Schools-Class *Repton* is seen here at Folkestone Junction in 1947 with a long passenger train. The Maunsell-designed engine was built at Eastleigh Works and released into service in May 1934. On Sunday, 30 December 1962, it was withdrawn. Two years previously, it had received a major service, so it was still in good condition. It was stored at Fratton until being moved to Eastleigh, and in 1964 it received a complete service. This was completed in 1967, at which time the purchaser had sold the engine to the Steamtown USA museum in Vermont. They, in turn, loaned *Repton* to the Cape Breton Steam Railway in Canada, where it worked a regular passenger service. In 1979 it was returned to the US, then in 1989, it was sold again and returned to the UK and the NYMR, where it was overhauled but found to be in good condition.

Owner Clifford Brown left the engine to the NYMR in his will. It is now operational on the NYMR.

▶ SR 4-6-2 21C135 *Shaftesbury*, Class West Country/Battle of Britain

West Country/Battle of Britain 21C135 *Shaftesbury* is seen at Folkestone Junction with 21C134 *Honiton* behind it in 1947. Bulleid designed them, and both engines were built at Brighton Works in July 1946. *Honiton* was rebuilt with the air-smoothed casing removed, but *Shaftesbury* was not. *Honiton*'s BR number was 34034, and *Shaftesbury*'s was 34035. *Honiton* was withdrawn in 1967, and *Shaftesbury* was withdrawn in 1963. Both engines were scrapped.

► SR 4-4-0 905 *Tonbridge*, Class V Schools

Robertsbridge station is seen here on 7 July 1935 with a long train. The Maunsell-designed engine was built at Eastleigh Works, going into service in May 1930. In October 1949, the number was changed to 30905. In 1958 it was fitted with a high-sided, self-trimming tender from a tender swap with 30932.

The locomotive was withdrawn from Basingstoke on Saturday, 9 December 1961 and scrapped at Eastleigh Works the following February. There is a presentation box containing a Royal Doulton plate with a picture of No. 905, and there is also a OO scale model of *Tonbridge* made by Hornby.

◄ SR 2-6-0 1840, Class N

Exeter St Davids station in 1937 as Class-N locomotive 1840 stands at the platform. The Maunsell-designed engine was built at Ashford Works in August 1924. When joining BR in September 1948, the number was changed to 31840. It was withdrawn on 7 September 1964 and scrapped in December that year.

◄ SR 2-6-0 A614, Class U

Bournemouth Central on 5 August 1939 and Maunsell engine No. 1614 is standing in the station. The locomotive was built at Brighton Works in July 1928 for the SR with the number A614. At nationalisation, the number changed under BR to 31614. It was withdrawn on Saturday, 23 November 1963 and scrapped two months later at Eastleigh Works.

▼ SR 4-6-2 21C9 *Shaw Savill*, Class Merchant Navy

Another look at Bulleid Pacific-engine 21C9 *Shaw Savill*, now standing single engine at Exeter Central in 1946. The West Country engine was built at Eastleigh Works in July 1942. Due to the war conditions and post-war austerity, the class locomotives were created using welding to cut the price. Eastleigh Works could not do this, so the first ten to receive welded fireboxes had them made in Glasgow by the North British Locomotive Company. The problem was that the air-smoothed casing was constructed with asbestos and BR removed that in the late 1950s. In the case of this engine, it was rebuilt in March 1957, when it lost the air-smoothed casing. On entering BR in August 1949, it received the number 35009. During their lives, the class members received the nickname 'Spam Cans' after the shape of the unrebuilt engines. Railwaymen called them 'Packets' after the first class member, which was named *Channel Packet*.

Shaw Savill was withdrawn on Monday, 7 September 1964 from Exmouth Junction after a total mileage of 1,127,452. It was then sold to Woodham Brothers scrapyard in Barry, where it remained until 1989. Then what was left of it was moved to the Brighton Railway Museum project at the Pullman Works. Soon after, the museum project failed, and *Shaw Savill* eventually ended up at the old Swindon Works as a sad static exhibit; the works then housed a Designer Village shopping complex. In 2003 the locomotive was bought by Ian Riley, who took it to his Bury works, where it lay partly dismantled until 2009.

Work has now commenced on the engine at Riley & Son Ltd at Heywood, Lancashire.

▲ SR 4-4-0 911 *Dover*, Class V Schools

V Schools-Class No. 911 *Dover* is here within the platforms of Battle station on 25 July 1935. The station is on the Hastings Line and serves the town of Battle; the Maunsell locomotive was built at Eastleigh Works and entered service in December 1932. On nationalisation, the number was changed to 30911. It was withdrawn on Sunday, 30 December 1962 and scrapped at Eastleigh Works in September 1963.

▲ SR 2-6-4T 1911, Class W

At Battersea shed in 1932, the crew of a large and robust
Maunsell tank engine pose for the camera. It was built at
Eastleigh Works in January 1932 for the SR with the number
1911. On nationalisation, it gained the BR identity 31911 and
was withdrawn on Saturday, 5 October 1963. It was scrapped in
April 1964 at Eastleigh Works.

4 THE GREAT WESTERN RAILWAY (GWR)

Parliament incorporated the original GWR in 1835, and until 1923 amalgamations mainly involved railway companies that the GWR was already supporting. But here we are concentrating on the GWR that became one of the Big Four under the Railways Act 1921.

The GWR was the only company to keep its original identity from before the 1921 Railways Act. It covered towns from Birkenhead to Penzance, with the workshops in Swindon, and was known as 'God's Wonderful Railway'. It was the only company to experiment very expensively with broad-gauge tracks, under the genius that was Isambard Kingdom Brunel. Eventually, the different gauges around the country were brought into line. This resulted in scrapyards full of broad-gauge engines and stock.

This list comprises eighteen of the most prominent companies drawn into the GWR in 1921, but not all of them; many small companies were drawn into the original GWR throughout the years of its existence.

Alexandra (Newport and South Wales) Docks Railway (ADR)
Barry Railway

Brecon and Merthyr Tydfil Junction Railway (B&MR)
Burry Port and Gwendraeth Valley Railway (BP&GVR)
Cambrian Railway
Cardiff Railway
Cleobury Mortimer and Ditton Priors Light Railway (CM&DPLR)
Llanelli and Mynydd Mawr Railway
Midland and South Western Junction Railway (M&SWJR)
Neath and Brecon Railway
Port Talbot Railway and Docks Company (PTR&D)
Powlesland and Mason
Shrewsbury and Chester Railway
Rhondda and Swansea Bay Railway
Rhymney Railway
South Wales Mineral Railway
Swansea Harbour Trust
Taff Vale Railway (TVR)

Some railways were not included in the Act at the time, such as the Somerset and Dorset Joint Railway (S&DJR) and London's Metropolitan Railway.

Locomotives from Other Companies Joining the Great Western Railway under the Grouping Act

Locomotives inducted from the pre-1921 GWR are listed as original GWR.

▼ Original GWR 0-6-0PT 1756, Class 1854

The first of our GWR locomotives began life as an original GWR locomotive. It was designed by William Dean as a saddle tank and built at Swindon Works in November 1892. It went into service that month with the number 1756, and in May 1908 it became part of the Rhondda and Swansea Bay Railway. In February 1918, it was rebuilt and converted to a pannier tank. On amalgamation, it became part of the GWR under the Railways Act 1921. It is seen here in Port Talbot on 7 July 1935. On 31 July 1946, it was withdrawn and scrapped soon after.

◄ **Barry Railway 0-6-0T 783, Class E**

A good turnout here for the camera as staff members pose with the engine and in the wagon behind. The locomotive was designed and built by Hudswell, Clarke & Co., going into service in January 1890. On amalgamation with the GWR, it retained the number 783. It was withdrawn on 30 August 1948 to be scrapped soon after.

► **Cambrian Railways 0-6-0 849, Class CMB1**

A mixed goods train crosses the road in Builth Wells station hauled by Herbert Jones-designed locomotive 849. Beyer, Peacock & Co. completed the locomotive on 30 November 1918, and on amalgamation into the GWR it retained the number and was withdrawn on 31 October 1954. None of the twelve locomotives of the class were preserved.

► **Original GWR 0-6-0PT 2104, Class 2021**

Tysley shed in Birmingham in 1930, and a rather smart original GWR pannier tank locomotive, No. 2104, stands over the pit. The locomotive was designed by Dean and built at Wolverhampton Works (Stafford Road). It went into service in March 1902 as a saddle tank locomotive. In July 1927, the engine was rebuilt, giving it a pannier tank. It was present at nationalisation but withdrawn from Birkenhead on Friday, 11 May 1951 and scrapped soon after.

◄ **Original GWR 4-6-0 4053** *Princess Alexandra*, **Class Star**

Shrewsbury shed on 3 May 1936 and one of the original GWR's powerful locomotives. It was designed by George Jackson Churchward for the original GWR and built at Swindon Works in June 1914. On amalgamation and through to BR, it retained the number 4053. On 11 September 1954, it was withdrawn from Stafford Road and scrapped at Swindon Works.

▲ Original GWR 4-6-0 4060 *Princess Beatrice*, Class Star

A nice, steam-era photo with period carriages, smoke-etched
bridge and one of Churchward's powerful locomotives. The location
is Torquay West in 1938, as Star-Class *Princess Beatrice* travels
past the signal box. The locomotive was built at Swindon Works
in July 1914 and released into service with the number 4060.
This was retained throughout its service, through amalgamation
and nationalisation. It was withdrawn from Bristol Bath Road on
11 October 1952 and scrapped at Swindon Works.

◄ **L&MMR 0-6-0ST 359** *Maud*, **Class LMM1**

Swansea East Dock is the location of this saddle tank locomotive, and the date is 7 July 1935. It was built by Manning Wardle for the Llanelli and Mynydd Mawr Railway, going into service in June 1917. No. 359 carries the name *Maud*, and the number was displayed throughout its amalgamation and nationalisation. It was withdrawn on 16 February 1954 and scrapped at Swindon Works.

◄ **Original GWR 0-6-0ST 2124, Class 2021**

This locomotive was designed by Dean and built at Wolverhampton Works (Stafford Road) as a saddle tank, as seen here at Oswestry station in June 1931. It carried the number 2124 throughout its service and was rebuilt in 1934 as a pannier tank. On 3 July 1950, it was withdrawn and scrapped after forty-seven years and two months' service.

When the Big Four came into being, the opportunity arose to create an eclectic mix of posters and advertising, giving a bit of colour to railway stations, train carriages and the company vans and trucks. There follows a selection of railway ephemera and posters from the Big Four.

(LMS images courtesy of Peter Tatlow, president of the
LMS Society, and Arnold Tortorella, society secretary)

LMS *High Guide*, 1929.

A 1939 timetable of LNER rail and shipping services to the Continent.

Coronation afternoon tea menu.

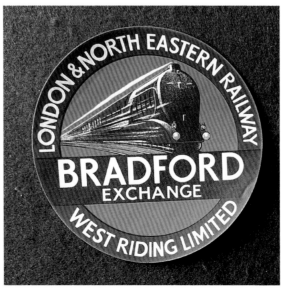

West Riding Limited luggage label, Bradford.

Coronation luggage label, Edinburgh.

The last LNER timetable for main-line services.

The last LNER timetable for suburban services from King's Cross.

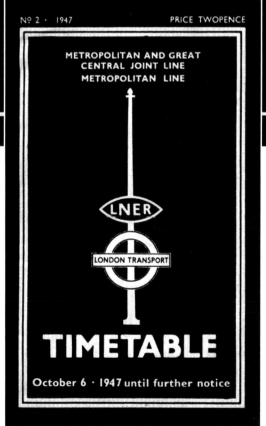

(LNER images courtesy of David Woodward of the LNER Society)

The last LNER timetable for suburban services from Marylebone.

Above and right: Silver Jubilee souvenir matches.

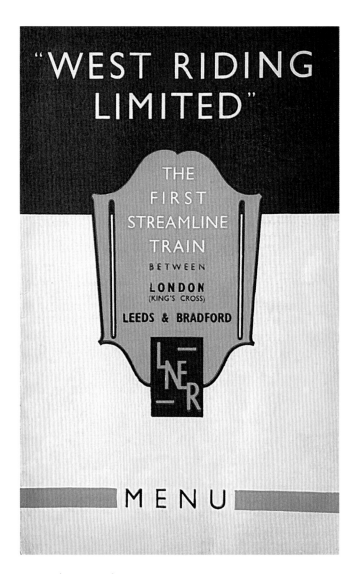

West Riding Limited menu cover.

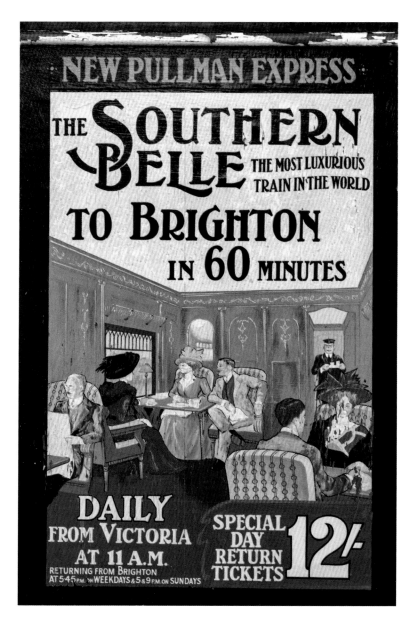

Historic SR poster advertising the Southern Belle service.
(Courtesy Mauritius Images GmbH/Alamy Stock Photo)

A vintage poster advertising SR connections to RMS *Queen Mary* passenger liner.
(Courtesy Rob Cole Photography/Alamy Stock Photo)

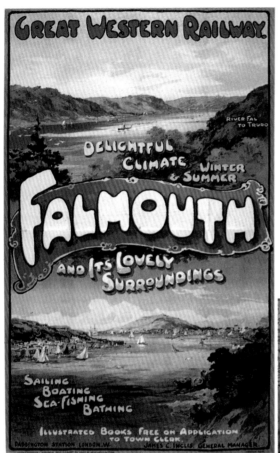

A Falmouth poster from GWR advertising the delights of holidaying in Cornwall. (Lordprice Collection/Alamy Stock Photo)

A vintage travel poster for GWR. (PD/Alamy Stock Photo)

 100 YEARS OF PROGRESS 1835 — 1935

▲ M&SWJR 4-4-0 1120, Class 1120

One member of this class of locomotives is seen here in Cheltenham Spa station with a period train in 1931. No. 1120 was built in April 1909 for the M&SWJR by the North British Locomotive Company. It was in a class of just nine locomotives known as Tyrrell 4-4-0s, constructed between 1905 and 1914. The M&SWJR's locomotive superintendent from 1903 to 1923 was James Tyrrell. It became part of the GWR on amalgamation, and it was rebuilt with five other class members between 1924 and 1929, giving them a taper boiler. Its last GWR shed was Swindon, from where it was withdrawn in August 1931 and scrapped soon after. The locomotive designer is not well known. He started as a clerk at Didcot in 1867, which led to a position with the GWR at Swindon. He worked his way to fireman and then driver, until in 1881, he left the GWR and moved to the M&SWJR in 1884, as a footplate man. From there, his career took off; he became manager of the carriage and wagon department, including the running department. Within three years, he took charge of the department as superintendent. He retired in 1923 and died on 13 March 1948, aged 94.

▲ **Cardiff Railway 0-6-0PT 682, Class CR 2**

Here we have a locomotive that was built as a saddle tank
engine. It was designed and built by Hudswell Clarke & Co. and
went into service on 29 February 1920 for Cardiff Railway with
the number 682. When taken over by the GWR in 1921, it was
reboilered and fitted with pannier tanks. It was withdrawn on
31 October 1953 from Cardiff East Dock, where it is seen here
on 20 June 1949.

◄ Original GWR 0-6-0PT 2772, Class 2721

Seen at Leamington Spa in September 1947 is a Dean pannier tank shunting engine built at Swindon Works for the original GWR in September 1900 as a saddle tank. After amalgamation, it was rebuilt by the GWR as a pannier tank locomotive and was withdrawn on 24 November 1949 from Leamington MPD.

► Original GWR 2-6-0 2639, Class 2600/Aberdare

Seen with long loose-coupled freight at Whitnash in Warwickshire in 1932 is a Dean locomotive. It was built at Swindon Works, going into service in June 1901 for the original GWR. The main job for this class of eighty locomotives was to haul coal trains between Aberdare and Swindon. On amalgamation, it retained its number, and it was withdrawn on 15 May 1946 and scrapped at Swindon Works.

▲ Original GWR 4-6-0 4011 *Knight of the Garter*, Class Star

A smart, powerful locomotive somewhat older than it looks is 4011 *Knight of the Garter*, stationary at Worcester shed on an unknown date. The Dean-designed locomotive was built at Swindon Works, going into service in March 1908. It retained the number after amalgamation and was withdrawn in November 1932 and scrapped at Swindon Works soon after.

► **Cambrian Railway 0-6-0 910, Class 1**

This locomotive spent most of its life at Oswestry, going into amalgamation and being withdrawn from the same depot. It was designed by Dean and built by Sharp, Stewart & Co., going into service in April 1865. It is seen here at Oswestry station in 1929 with a train of cattle wagons and was withdrawn from here in May 1935, then scrapped soon after.

◄ **Original GWR 0-6-2T 322, Class TV-A**

No. 322 is seen here at Barry shed in 1948 with a steam crane to the rear. The locomotive was designed by John Cameron, the carriage and wagon superintendent of the TVR in Cardiff. It was built by Hawthorn, Leslie & Co. of Newcastle upon Tyne and released into service in January 1915. The number 322 was carried throughout amalgamation and nationalisation, and it was withdrawn from Abercynon on 30 October 1954.

► **CM&DPLR 0-6-0PT 29, Class CMDP**

Quite a rare photograph of one of only two
locomotives owned by the CM&DPLR. The
two locomotives owned by the company on
being absorbed into the GWR in 1922 were
numbered 28 and 29, and 29 is seen here as it
stands at the platform at Kidderminster Halt in
1931. It was designed and built by Manning
Wardle in August 1908 as a saddle tank
locomotive. Under the GWR, it was rebuilt
with a new boiler and pannier tanks, becoming
an 0-6-0PT. It was withdrawn on 28 February
1954.

◄ **SHT 0-4-0ST 5, Class SHT-1**

This locomotive was built by Andrew Barclay,
Sons & Co. of Kilmarnock for the Swansea
Harbour Trust in April 1904. It is seen here
at Swansea East Dock shed on 7 July 1935.
When released into service, it carried the
number 5 but this was changed to 701
when absorbed into the GWR. On 25 June
1948, under BR, the number was changed to
1140. At this time, the locomotive was at the
Caerphilly Locomotive Works, the only main
railway works in Wales, which closed in 1963
and is now an industrial estate. No. 1140
was withdrawn from Swansea East Dock on
31 May 1958 and was scrapped two months
later at Swindon Works.

◄ **Original GWR 2-6-0 2608, Class 2600/Aberdare**

The year is 1937 as Dean-designed locomotive 2608 hauls a long, mixed freight near Harbury in Warwickshire. The locomotive was built at Swindon Works for the original GWR, going into service in January 1906. It was withdrawn on Friday, 19 October 1945 and scrapped at Swindon Works two months later.

► **Original GWR 4-4-0 270 *Trevithick*, Class Duke**

At Aberystwyth shed on 22 August 1934 with a tender full of coal is Duke-Class locomotive 3264 *Trevithick*. It was designed by Dean and built at Swindon Works, going into service on 6 June 1896 with the pre-1921 number 270. In December 1912, the identity was changed to 3264. Then, on induction into the GWR, this became 9064 but only until 31 December 1949. It was then withdrawn from Gloucester Horton Road for disposal.

▲ SHT 0-6-0ST 1085, Class SHT-5

Sitting quietly at Danygraig shed within the Swansea Harbour
complex on 7 July 1935 is a saddle tank locomotive built for the
Swansea Harbour Trust. It was built and designed by Peckett &
Co. in April 1912, then released with the number 1085. It spent its
time in service at the Swansea East Dock and was withdrawn on
31 January 1951.

▲ **M&SWJR 2-4-0 1335, Class MSWJ**

Newbury station in Berkshire is where we see one of a small
class of three locomotives built for the M&SWJR. No. 1335
was designed and built by Dubs & Co., going into service
on 1 January 1894. It was given the number 1335, which
it carried throughout amalgamation and nationalisation. It
was withdrawn from Reading on 30 September 1952 after
fifty-eight years and eight months in service.

◄ **Original GWR 4-4-0 3480 *County of Stafford*, Class County**

Passing through Bentley Heath near Solihull in 1928 is an exceptionally clean member of the Churchward-designed County Class. In this case, 3837 *County of Stafford*. It was hauling a mixed freight. The locomotive was built at Swindon Works, going into service in October 1904 with the number 3480. On amalgamation, 3837 was applied. It was withdrawn in March 1931 and scrapped shortly after.

► **Original GWR 0-4-2T 1159, Class 517**

Sitting quietly in a clean condition on 23 June 1935 at Swindon Works is tank engine No. 1159. George Armstrong designed it for the GWR. It was built at Armstrong Works (Stafford Road) and went into service in January 1876. After a long, hard service life of over seventy-one years, it was withdrawn from Oxford, still with the number 1159, on 22 August 1947.

► Original GWR 0-4-2T 1473 *Fair Rosamund*, Class 517

Here we have another 517-Class tank engine, 1473. It was designed by George Armstrong and built at Wolverhampton Works (Stafford Road), going into service in May 1883. It is seen here at Kidlington station in Oxfordshire in 1930. In 1898 it was named *Fair Rosamund* to work a Royal Train on the Oxford to Woodstock branch. 'Fair Rosamund' was Rosamund Clifford; she lived at Woodstock in the twelfth century and was the mistress of King Henry II. The locomotive spent most of its long life at Oxford, carrying the number 1473 throughout its service, and was withdrawn in August 1935.

◄ Original GWR 4-4-0 4104 *Calendula*, Class Flower

It is 1930 and hauling a stopping train to Oxford is Dean-designed clean locomotive 4152 *Calendula*. It was built at Swindon Works, going into service in May 1908 with the number 4104. In December 1912, the number was changed to 4152, and it was withdrawn in September 1928 and scrapped soon after.

► Original GWR Steam Rail Motor 73

The original GWR built ninety-nine steam
rail motors and numbered them from
1 to 99 between 1903 and 1908. Shown
here is one built in 1906 at the Gloucester
Railway Carriage and Wagon Co. No. 73
was withdrawn as a rail motor in June 1933.
The following year, on 24 February 1934, it
was converted into an autocoach with the
number 202. On 24 March 1956, it was
withdrawn as a trailer car and scrapped. It is
seen here at Exeter shed in 1932.

◄ Original GWR 2-4-0 3210, Class Barnum

An ancient Barnum-Class engine stands at
the platform in Crewe station, the far reaches
of the old GWR. The date is 6 June 1935.
No. 3210 was designed by Dean and built
at Swindon Works in May 1889. The name
Barnum comes from one of the class's duties,
which was to carry Barnum and Bailey's circus.
No. 3210 was withdrawn from Wellington
shed in Shropshire in May 1947 and scrapped
at Swindon Works.

▲ **Original GWR 2-4-0 3251, Class 3232**

Crewe Gresty Road shed and the crew pose for the camera as they stand by their newly cleaned old locomotive in the 1920s. It was designed by Dean and built at Swindon Works, going into service in July 1893. It was withdrawn in April 1930 and scrapped soon after.

▲ Original GWR 4-4-0 3418 *Earl of Cork*, Class Bulldog

Seen here at Shrewsbury station in 1931 is the gently steaming
3366 *Earl of Cork*, a single-engine member of the Bulldog Class.
It was designed by Dean and built at Swindon Works, going into
service in February 1903 with the number 3418. In 1912 the
number was changed to 3366, the identity that it would retain
throughout amalgamation. In 1936 the name *Earl of Cork* was
removed. It was withdrawn from Chester on 24 April 1948 and
scrapped at Swindon Works.

► Original GWR 4-4-0 3449 *Reading*, Class Bulldog

Hauling a light freight through Swan Village station Staffordshire (closed 1972) on 7 July 1930 is a Bulldog-Class locomotive. It was designed by Dean and built at Swindon Works, going into service in October 1903. At this time it carried the number 3449 and the name *Reading*. In December 1912, it received the new number 3387, and in May 1927 the name was removed. This was because some passengers took it to be the destination! It was withdrawn on 6 December 1934 and scrapped at Swindon Works.

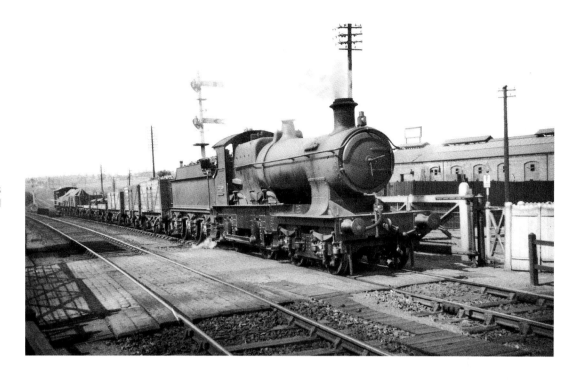

◄ Original GWR 4-4-0 3276 *Dartmoor*, Class Duke

Standing cold at Didcot shed in 1931 is another Dean engine that was built at Swindon Works and entered service in December 1896 with the number 3276 and named *Dartmoor*. In 1912 the number was changed to 3269. It was withdrawn from Oswestry shed in April 1937 and scrapped at Swindon Works shortly after.

Locomotives Built by the Great Western Railway from 1922 to 1949

▲ GWR 4-6-0 6912 *Helmster Hall*, Class Hall

At Oxford station now in 1948 with one of Collett's fine Hall-Class engines. It was built at Swindon Works, going into service on 30 January 1941. The same name and number were carried throughout its BR days, and it was withdrawn on 14 February 1964 and scrapped later at Hayes of Bridgend.

◀ GWR 0-6-0 2259, Class 2251

Here we have another Collett locomotive in the form of 2259. It was built at Swindon Works, entering service in April 1930. The number was retained during BR days, and it was withdrawn and scrapped at Swindon Works on 31 May 1959. The photograph was taken at Bala station in 1948 with a pick-up goods train.

▶ GWR 2-6-2T 4122, Class 5101

GWR Large Prairie Tank 4122 is stopped at Helsby station awaiting the off; the date is 2 August 1947. It was designed by Collett and built at Swindon Works, going into service on 1 January 1938. It was withdrawn from Neyland on 15 June 1964 and scrapped at Birds of Morriston.

▲ **GWR 4-6-0 6014 *King Henry VII*, Class King**

Part-streamlined 6014 *King Henry VII* is seen here passing Leamington Spa with a passenger train in 1939. The Collett locomotive was built as part of the most powerful class in the GWR at Swindon Works, going into service in May 1928. Until 1935 it was, along with the rest of the class, an attractive locomotive. Then, in 1935, it was decided to streamline it to make it go faster and use less coal. The result was that it was turned into a total ugly duckling of an engine. As time went on and criticism mounted, bits were taken off, leaving the ugly bulbous nose. By January 1943, it had all gone – well, except the V-shaped cab, which was not a problem. It was withdrawn on Friday, 21 September 1962 and scrapped on 7 March 1963 at Cox and Danks scrapyard at Oldbury.

◄ GWR 4-6-0 6847 *Tidmarsh Grange*, Class Grange

The smoky interior of Birmingham Snow Hill station hosts Grange-Class engine *Tidmarsh Grange*. It was designed by Collett and released into service on 20 October 1937. After twenty-eight years, it was withdrawn on Friday, 3 December 1965 and scrapped at J. Buttigiegs of Newport four months later. One of the nameplates is now displayed at the station museum at Bishop's Lydeard on the West Somerset Railway.

◄ GWR Diesel Railcar No. 34

A look at a GWR diesel railcar, this time one that only carried express parcels, at Paddington station in 1948. It was built for this duty at Swindon Works, going into service on 15 September 1941 with a capacity to carry 10 tons. It was withdrawn in September 1960, then scrapped. Hornby Models have made a scale model of No. 34.

▲ **GWR 0-4-2T 5801, Class 5800**

A member of a small class of Collett tank engines, No. 5801 was built
at Swindon Works, going into service on 4 January 1933 for the GWR.
It served mainly at Brecon and Machynlleth and was withdrawn on
9 September 1958, then sold for scrap on 2 March 1959 to Morkot
Ltd of Caerphilly. It is seen here in 1946 at Dovey Junction.

► GWR 4-6-0 1024 *County of Pembroke,* Class County

Seen here at Leamington Spa, in June 1948, is a powerful Frederick Hawksworth-designed locomotive that was built just in time to join the GWR before BR took over. It was built at Swindon Works, going into service on Wednesday, 9 January 1947. It was withdrawn on Wednesday, 8 April 1964 from Swindon and scrapped at Swindon Works two months later. None of the class of thirty locomotives was saved, but a project is under way to build a replica with the name *County of Glamorgan*; 1024 has donated its reverser to the project.

◄ GWR Diesel Railcar No. 26

Another look at a GWR diesel railcar, in this case first introduced in 1934, one of the successful classes introduced by the company. Some were bigger than others, and some hauled passenger carriages, carried parcels, and even had buffet facilities. No. 26, seen here, was built at Swindon Works in 1940/41. It seated forty-eight passengers, and had further seating in the attached carriage. The railcar was withdrawn in October 1962 and scrapped shortly after. It is seen here with an attached carriage at Oxford station in 1948.

► GWR 4-6-0 4094 *Dynevor Castle*,
Class Castle

A Collett-designed powerful locomotive of the
Castle Class, No. 4094 *Dynevor Castle*, is seen
here light engine at Hereford station in March
1938. It was built at Swindon Works, going
into service on Friday, 6 June 1926 at Old
Oak Common. After thirty-five years and nine
months, it was withdrawn from Carmarthen
on 23 March 1962. Scrapping followed at
Swindon Works the following month.

◄ GWR 4-6-0 1013 *County of Dorset*,
Class County

Exeter St Davids station on a dull day on
30 August 1947 as Hawksworth-designed
County-Class *County of Dorset* stands
at the head of a long rake of period
carriages awaiting the off. It was built at
Swindon Works, going into service on
11 February 1946. After a relatively short
life of eighteen years and five months, it was
withdrawn from Swindon and scrapped in
December 1964 at Cashmore's of Newport.

◄ GWR 4-6-0 7810 *Draycott Manor*, Class Manor

Birmingham Snow Hill station in 1947 is where we see a member of the Manor Class: 7810 *Draycott Manor*. Designed by Collett and built at Swindon Works for the GWR, it went into service on 10 December 1938. It was withdrawn on 26 September 1964 and scrapped at Birds of Swansea.

► GWR 4-6-0 4954 *Plaish Hall*, Class Hall

At London's Paddington station as Hall-Class locomotive *Plaish Hall* leaves with a train. It was designed by Collett and built at Swindon Works, going into service in August 1929. After a service life of thirty-five years, it was withdrawn from Wolverhampton Stafford Road on Saturday, 14 November 1964 and scrapped at Cashmore's of Great Bridge.

◄ **GWR 4-6-0 100** *A1 Lloyds,* **Class Castle**

Steaming past Leamington Spa station in 1936 is a Churchward rebuild from the Star-Class locomotive 4009 *Shooting Star*, which was originally built on 18 May 1907. On 9 April 1925, it was taken into Swindon Works under Churchward and completely transformed into a Castle-Class locomotive, No. 4009. In January 1936, it was renumbered A1, and the following month it was given the number 100 and name *A1 Lloyds* that is seen here and was carried to the end. The number 100 is on the cab side with A1 beneath, both on brass plates. During the 1940s, it was fitted for oil firing. On Monday, 5 March 1950, it was withdrawn from Swindon and scrapped there in the same month, the first of the class to be withdrawn.

◄ **GWR 0-6-0PT 5725, Class 5700 57xx**

Snow Hill in Birmingham in 1929, and a quite new pannier tank shunter is working in the station. Leaning from the door is the fireman. The engine was designed by Collett and built at the North British Locomotive Company in Glasgow, going into service in January 1929. The class was one of the most prolific on BR. Some went to London Transport on withdrawal, but this was not one of them; it was withdrawn from Chester on 30 September 1958 and scrapped at Swindon Works the following month.

▲ **GWR 2-6-0 6389, Class 4300 43xx**

Just creeping in on amalgamation is a locomotive in excellent condition. It was designed by Churchward and built at Robert Stephenson & Hawthorns Ltd, going into service in October 1921. It is seen here at Warwick in 1937 and was withdrawn on 21 September 1960 from Neyland. On 25 March 1961, it was scrapped at Swindon Works.

▲ **GWR 2-6-2T 5163, Class 3101**

Large Prairie Tank 5163 passes through Claverdon in Warwickshire (still a working station) in August 1939. The Collett-designed locomotive was built at Swindon Works, going into service in November 1930. It was withdrawn on 2 November 1959 and scrapped at Cashmore's of Newport.

▲ GWR 2-6-2T 5509, Class 4575

Bridgenorth in August 1934 and a Large Prairie Tank 5509 is engaged on shunting duties with four cattle wagons as part of a mixed train. Designed by Collett and built at Swindon Works, it went into service in October 1927. It was withdrawn on 21 December 1961 and scrapped at Cashmore's of Newport in June 1962.

◄ GWR Diesel Railcar No. W20

This railcar was built at Swindon Works in 1940; it was one of the last to be built for the GWR. When built, it received the number W20 and, when in BR, W20W. It was withdrawn from service in 1960 and put into storage. After this, it was bought by the Kent and East Sussex Railway (KESR) at Tenterden. Six years were spent restoring it, and it was the first KESR locomotive to enter revenue-earning service in February 1974. After six years, it was found to have serious problems; it is still being rebuilt at the time of writing. It is seen here on 3 July 1953, leaving Dorchester in BR's service.

► GWR 4-6-0 4978 *Westwood Hall*, Class Hall

The driver looks from his cab as 4978 *Westwood Hall* stands at the platform at Basingstoke on 29 July 1933. The Collett locomotive was built at Swindon Works in February 1930, and after thirty-four years and seven months it was withdrawn on 21 September 1964 and scrapped three months later at R.S. Hayes/Birds, Tremains Yard in Bridgend.

▼ GWR 4-6-0 6003 *King George IV*, Class King

At a busy Wolverhampton Stafford Road shed on 1 October 1923 stands a majestic member of the 6000 King Class. It was designed by Collett and built at Swindon Works, going into service in July 1927. A career of thirty-four years and eleven months followed before withdrawal on 19 June 1962 and scrapping at Swindon Works three months later.

▲ **GWR 0-6-0 8700, Class 5700**

Photographed at Old Oak Common on 22 April 1934, 9700
was designed by Collett and built by Beyer, Peacock & Co. in
February 1931 with the number 8700. On 31 January 1934
it was renumbered 9700 and was withdrawn from Old Oak
Common on 10 March 1964, to be scrapped at Swindon
Works two months later.

► GWR 2-8-0 4705, Class 47xx

No. 4705 was designed by Churchward for the GWR as one of the first locomotives to be built for the new company. It was built in 1922 at Swindon Works, going into service in April, and is seen here at Tyseley shed. The small but powerful class of nine locomotives was originally planned for heavy overnight fast freight work. Hence, they received the nickname 'Night Owls'. This never stopped them from being allocated heavy relief passenger services during the summer months.

Their limited use and heavy weight meant that the class collectively had a relatively low mileage. However, 4705 travelled the longest total mileage of the class at 1,656,564 miles. It was withdrawn on 2 December 1963 at Old Oak Common and scrapped in March 1964.

None of the class members were saved, but the Great Western Society have decided to build the next locomotive in the sequence, 4709, using new and recovered parts of scrapped engines. The planned name is *Night Owl*.

◄ GWR 4-6-0 6832 *Brockton Grange*, Class Grange

Whitchurch Black Bridge in 1938 and Grange-Class *Brockton Grange* thunders through with a rake of ex-LSWR stock. The locomotive was designed by Collett and built at Swindon Works, going into service on 13 August 1937. It was withdrawn on 15 January 1964 and scrapped by Cohens of Morriston five months later.

◀ GWR 0-4-2T 4843, Class 1400

Blenheim and Woodstock station (closed in 1954) in 1947, and a solitary lady awaits her train. Standing at the platform hooked up to an autotrain carriage is a Collett tank engine. It was built at Swindon Works with the number 4843, going into service on 8 April 1935. While at the Stafford Road Factory on 26 October 1946, it was renumbered 1443. On 27 June 1957, it was withdrawn, and scrapping followed at Swindon Works three months later.

▶ GWR 2-6-2T 4590, Class 4575

Marlborough station (closed completely in 1964) in 1936, and the platform is filled with passengers awaiting a train in the other direction. Many soldiers are among them, as are several children; they could possibly be saying goodbye to their fathers as they return to barracks. Although it was still peacetime, soon the clouds of war would descend. This was another Collett engine built at Swindon Works, being released into service in March 1927. These small Prairie tanks were very popular with preservation groups, but this one was not so lucky and was withdrawn on 24 October 1948 and scrapped at Swindon Works four months later.

◄ GWR 4-6-0 6026 *King John*, Class King

Steaming through Warwick station in 1938 with a long train of carriages is the King-Class locomotive *King John*. The engine is spotless. The Collett-designed engine was built at Swindon Works, going into service in July 1930. These heavy and powerful engines were used on the top-link services, such as the Cornish Riviera. When these express trains needed to go beyond Plymouth, the engine had to be changed to a Castle or Hall, the King Class being too heavy for the Royal Albert Bridge over the River Tamar. No. 6026 was withdrawn on 12 September 1962. On Saturday, 12 December 1963, it was scrapped at Swindon Works after travelling a total of 1,622,350 miles.

► GWR 4-6-0 6005 *King George II*, Class King

Swan Village, West Bromwich, and King-Class *King George II* passes over the level crossing with a long passenger train on 7 July 1934. Collett designed and built it at Swindon Works, and it went into service the same month. After clocking up 1,679,275 miles, it was withdrawn on Tuesday, 20 December 1962 and scrapped a year later at Cashmore's of Great Bridge.

► GWR 4-6-0 4901 *Adderley Hall*, Class Hall

The second locomotive in the 259-strong class designed by Collett and built at Swindon was 4901 *Adderley Hall*. It is seen here hauling a passenger train at Penzance on 25 August 1936. It was withdrawn from Oxley on 16 September 1960 and scrapped at Swindon Works in December that year.

◄ GWR 4-6-0 5017 *St Donat's Castle*, Class Castle

Seen here at Swindon Works is 5017 *The Gloucestershire Regiment 28th 61st*. The date is 11 May 1954, and the locomotive has just been renamed. The original name was *St Donat's Castle*. However, it was chosen to have a name change to commemorate the excellent work of the Glosters during the Korean War. The Collett-designed locomotive was built at Swindon Works, going into service at Taunton on 11 July 1932. It was withdrawn from Gloucester Horton Road on 21 September 1962 and scrapped three months later at Cashmore's of Newport.

▲ **Stourbridge Junction Shed**

This railway shed was built by the original GWR and opened in 1870 as a four-road shed constructed in brick. On amalgamation in 1923, it joined the re-formed GWR. It is seen here in 1952. It was situated on the west side of Stourbridge Junction station. On 11 July 1966, the shed was closed to steam locomotives, although diesel multiple units were serviced there until 6 May 1968. The shed was demolished soon after, and a housing estate has now taken its place.

EPILOGUE

As we commemorate the 100 years since the Railways Act 1921, better known as the Grouping Act, it is timely to briefly look at what happened after that period of change. The number of railway companies was vastly reduced. Many ancient classes of locomotives belonging to the companies that became part of the Grouping Act were withdrawn, and more modern steam and electric locomotives assumed their places in the new Big Four. The years that followed 1921 saw the advent of powerful classes of locomotives built by such luminaries as Gresley, Stanier, Collett, Dean, Bulleid, Churchward, Thompson, Urie, Maunsell and others, who provided the designs that saw the country grow in industrial strength.

The rail companies also suffered through the Second World War, when services were again much in demand. They were an essential part of the war effort. In 1949, as at the end of the First World War, the railway was in disarray, mainly due to the inability during the war to maintain the usual high standard. The Labour Government assumed power and introduced a storm of nationalisations. A few actually worked, some were useful, some were silly – Thomas Cooke travel agents and road transport, to name but two.

The railways never really became profitable; excellent prototype diesel engines like 10000 and 10001 were built and worked quite well, but that was in the late 1940s. Experimental steam engines were also trialled and while some worked, some, like Bulleid's Leader, did not. However, the decision was made to stick with steam, and some excellent standard classes emerged. There followed Beeching and his savage cuts at the behest of Ernest Marples, the Minister of Transport, who just happened to be a motorway man. This helped lead to the end of steam in 1968. It did not improve BR's prospects, and eventually, privatisation came along. There are mixed feelings about this, and it had its ups and downs; some believed that if the public money that was spent on privatisation could have been given to BR, it could have worked.

At the time of writing, a form of nationalisation is being reconsidered by the government. The amount of traffic on the roads is becoming a problem. Is the HS2 rail development going to be another white elephant? I would surmise that the future is the railways, for different reasons than at the time of the Big Four amalgamation. Many people can see plenty of reasons to upgrade the network both for goods and passengers, but there is not much faith in the outrageously expensive HS2 among the silent majority. The whole system is ready for another overhaul.

It is now 100 years since the Railways Act 1921, which became law in January 1923, and this book commemorates that auspicious period when the railways went on to serve the country from that point to the present day. The future of the railways is secured, and the Big Four have left their mark.

The many preserved lines have gone from strength to strength, becoming more and more popular with all ages. The working steam locomotives bring back happy memories for the enthusiasts who were there and people of all ages who have grown to enjoy the heady smell of smoke, steam and oil, together with the sight and sound of a hard-working railway engine.

So, I hope you enjoyed this book's journey from the locomotives of the late nineteenth century through to 1923 and onwards to BR with a little peek at privatisation. Jeremy and I have certainly enjoyed compiling it. Roll on to the next significant change in rail travel, the next Grouping Act, and the overhauling of the present rail infrastructure.

Remembering
STEAM

The End of British Rail Steam in Photographs

PAUL HURLEY AND PHIL BRAITHWAITE

978 0 7509 8427 0